The Sentence Book

Second Edition

LEE A. JACOBUS

University of Connecticut

The Sentence Book

Second Edition

Harcourt Brace Jovanovich, Inc.

New York · San Diego · Chicago · San Francisco · Atlanta
London · Sydney · Toronto

Preface

The purpose of the second edition of *The Sentence Book* remains the same as the first: to help students learn to write clear, well-organized sentences. Students are guided step-by-step through mastery of the basic parts of the sentence and then are taught how to avoid the pitfalls of much student writing. Each element of the sentence, from the simple subject to the simple predicate through subject, predicate, and pronoun agreement, is discussed in a separate unit. Familiar problems, like the sentence fragment and the run-on sentence, are also treated in individual units. This presentation, which is simple, flexible, and employs traditional terminology, allows *The Sentence Book* to be used as a core text in composition courses or as a supplement to review grammar and composition. But above all, *The Sentence Book* is a writing book, not a fill-in-the-blanks book. From the beginning, students write their own sentences and, later on, build strings of exercise sentences into narrative or descriptive paragraphs. One instructor congratulates his students for being co-authors with me, because by the end of the term they have written almost as much in the book as I have. This is only fair, since the book is for writers, and what it teaches is writing.

The second edition reinforces this emphasis on writing with new instruction in proofreading the sentence and the paragraph. In the section on proofreading the sentence, students are taught how to review their work and improve it, while in the section on proofreading the paragraph they learn how to achieve unity and coherence in larger units of writing. A new section on sentence combining and sentence analysis brings together the principles of the book and shows how they can be used to create clear sentences. Also included in this edition are units on sentence patterning and learning from the writing of professionals. In these units, students are asked to write sentences that fulfill specific models in order to demonstrate the effectiveness of sentence variety and the placement of important elements of meaning within a sentence. The opportunity to analyze the sentence patterns of good writers helps students see the usefulness of learning the basic parts of the sentence. By following these methods, students often surprise themselves with the professional quality of their writing.

As in the first edition, Punctuation Pointers appear throughout the text and treat common punctuation problems. This results in teaching punctuation where it is pertinent, a method that is pedagogically more effective than treating it in an isolated chapter. Pointers on composition also treat specific issues, such as the difference between the restrictive and nonrestrictive clause, as they arise.

Although the progressive nature of *The Sentence Book* allows for self-instruction, the book is best used in the classroom where the instructor can reinforce basic principles and clarify difficult points. Students can then take advantage of the numerous opportunities provided throughout the text to review their own writing in light of these basic principles. In addition, three tests, which may be used in any of several ways, are supplied at the end of the book. The first is a diagnostic test designed to help instructor and student see which areas treated by the book will need the closest and most immediate attention. The second test examines students for their understanding of the principles developed in Section I: Basic Parts and Basic Problems. The third test focuses on the construction of clauses and phrases covered in Section II: Principles of Subordination. The tests can all be used as diagnostic tests, or as achievement tests, or, if the instructor does not wish to use them as tests, they can be used to supplement the exercise material in the book itself.

A great many people have contributed to this revision. Some have written detailed reviews that have proved invaluable. For their help I would like to thank: Richard H. Anderson, Hartnell College, Salinas, California; Thomas Bonner, Jr., Xavier University of Louisiana; Michael Clark, University of Michigan; Patrick W. Conner, West Virginia University; Elizabeth F. Cooper, University of Houston, Downtown College; Rosalie Hewitt, Northern Illinois University; Terese C. Karmel, Eastern Connecticut State College; James Mackillop, State University College, Utica, New York; and David Van Becker, San Jose State University. Others have worked with me in the University of Connecticut Summer Program, which was the inspiration for the first edition of the book. Their advice has been immeasurably helpful. Finally, a special thanks to Judith Davis Miller, who used *The Sentence Book* in the program, and who helped produce this revision. In many ways, her insights and her work were instrumental in making this revision possible.

Lee A. Jacobus

Contents

SECTION **II**

Principles
of Subordination 55

SECTION **III**

Principles
of Coordination   93

SECTION VII

Tests and Evaluations 179

The
Sentence
Book

Second Edition

SECTION I

Basic Parts and Basic Problems

1 The Simple Subject

Every complete sentence has at least two parts: the simple subject and the simple predicate (a verb whose action is complete). The simple subject can be the single word or words that name the main person, place, thing, or idea of the sentence. Usually we find the subject at the beginning of the sentence rather than at the end. Therefore most sentences we write and speak look like this:

$$\boxed{\text{subject}} + \boxed{\text{predicate}}$$

This pattern is basic to English speech and English writing and should be mastered quickly.

The simple subject is always a noun or a pronoun. Nouns can be identified in three basic ways.

The proper noun

Since the subject is the name of something, any proper name (the name of a specific person, place, or thing) can be the subject of a sentence.

1. Tammy Wynette
2. John Wayne
3. Rita
4. Henry Kissinger
5. Reggie Jackson
6. Joseph Anthony Rosado
7. Aunt Helen
8. Henry Ford
9. Anwar Sadat
10. Chris Evert

There are other kinds of proper names that can serve as the simple subject of a sentence. The following list gives names of movies, buildings, poems, plays, short stories, books, TV shows, businesses, and institutions.

1. *Star Wars*
2. *Gone with the Wind*
3. *A Raisin in the Sun*
4. "The Pit and the Pendulum"
5. Shea Stadium
6. *Guinness Book of World Records*
7. The Bank of America
8. Manchester Community College
9. "Casey at the Bat"
10. *The Carol Burnett Show*

▶ **PUNCTUATION POINTER**

The examples above show that the first letter of each word of a proper name is capitalized. The shorter words in a title, such as "in" or "the," are not capitalized unless they come first or last. The names

---

of books, films, and TV shows are in italics, as in this example: *Star Wars*; poems and short stories are enclosed in quotation marks: "Casey at the Bat," "The Lottery."

In the following spaces, give the proper names of any people, movies, books, TV shows, buildings, places, businesses, or schools you have heard about.

1. _____   6. _____

2. _____   7. _____

3. _____   8. _____

4. _____   9. _____

5. _____   10. _____

Now take a minute to see if you have used capitals where they are needed and have underlined the names of books, movies, and TV shows. Be sure you have used quotation marks for short stories and poems.

The common noun

There are many names of things and activities that are not proper nouns. These nouns name a thing or an activity that you can see, hear, taste, touch, or smell, but they do not pertain only to a single person or thing. For instance, Ralph Ellison is the name of a specific man, not a general group of men; but Ellison is a writer, and the word "writer" is a common noun, since it is a name given to many people. The list below offers some common nouns, all of which can be used as simple subjects in a sentence.

1. cowboys   6. television set
2. stairs   7. joke
3. music   8. olive oil
4. perfume   9. passageway
5. stories   10. remarks

A common noun does not need a capital letter at its beginning because it names a general class of things. Nor does it require italics.

Add your own common nouns in the spaces provided below. Be sure each is the name of a thing or an activity you can see, hear, taste, touch, or smell, and that it is not a name that is given only to a single person or thing.

1. _____   6. _____

2. _____   7. _____

3. _____   8. _____

4. _____   9. _____

5. _____   10. _____

Now check to see that you have not capitalized any of these common nouns.

The abstract noun

The nouns we have been discussing are names given to people, places, or things that can be seen or heard. Even businesses are in a given place and hire workers who work in buildings with the business name on them. But when we describe things that cannot be seen or heard or in any way observed directly by our five senses, we are describing something that is abstract. The word "abstract" only means that we are talking about something that can be thought of or felt emotionally, but that cannot be seen in the way we can see a person or an object or a film. Yet even abstract things, such as human emotions or words that describe a condition of people or things, can be nouns, and in turn can be simple subjects. Following is a list of emotions or conditions of people or things. Like common nouns, abstract nouns are not capitalized unless they begin a sentence.

1. love   6. freedom
2. irritation   7. longing
3. surprise   8. privacy
4. hesitancy   9. courtesy
5. envy   10. destruction

Below, write your own list of abstract nouns that are emotions or that describe the condition of people, places, or things.

1. _____   6. _____

2. _____   7. _____

3. _____   8. _____

4. _____   9. _____

5. _____   10. _____

Check the list to be sure that you have not included proper nouns or names of things or activities you can see, hear, taste, touch, or smell.

2 The Subject with Adjective Modifiers

Most of the sentences we speak or write do not have simple subjects. They have subjects that use words or groups of words, called adjective modifiers, to make a fuller statement or to describe, make clear, or somehow limit the meaning of the simple subject. The pattern below shows the general way in which this is done.

> simple subject: the woman
> adjective modifier: married
> simple subject with adjective modifier: the married woman

The adjective modifier helps identify the woman in question. Since there are a great many married women, we might have to be more exact by adding another modifier:

> the married woman in apartment C

Now the modifiers make the simple subject even more clearly identified. Note that the modifiers can come both before and after the subject.

Each time we add a modifier that tells us more about who, where, when, how, why, which, or what, we describe the simple subject more fully, as in the following examples:

> friend
> my friend
> my only friend
> my only friend from back home
> my only male friend from back home

The examples below show a number of basic patterns we can use in developing the simple subject. In each case the adjective modifiers make the subject more clear, more exact in meaning. Ask yourself what each modifier does. What does it tell you about the simple subject? Notice that the simple subject is underlined.

1. Linda Jenkins from security
2. Jasper, both thoughtful and intelligent,
3. Zelda's friend with the Toronado
4. Last at bat but first on base, Reggie Jackson
5. James Baldwin, significant among American writers,
6. Mary Pickford, legendary film star,
7. everyone's happiness
8. unpleasant memories
9. the last angry man
10. The World Trade Towers, the tallest buildings in New York,

---

▶ **PUNCTUATION POINTER**

When the modifier expresses an idea that *is* the subject, and actually restates or equals it, we set that modifier off with commas. The technical term for this modifier is appositive. Groups of words used in apposition need commas. Such is the case in example 6 above, which might be described in this way:

> Mary Pickford = legendary film star

The modifiers in examples 2, 5, and 10 are also in apposition with their simple subjects. Notice that they are set off with commas

---

Adjective modifiers always add descriptive information to the simple subject or identify it. But note very carefully: adjective modifiers do not make the subject do anything. This is extremely important because once the subject is put into action, we are not building a subject with adjective modifiers; we are building a sentence, with a subject and predicate.

Use the simple subjects that follow and add your own modifiers. You may add them before the subject, after it, or both.

1. _____ Montgomery Ward _____

2. _____ ideas _____

3. _____ camera _____

4. _____ silence _____

5. _____ Liza _____

6. _____ Cleveland _____

7. _____ light bulbs _____

8. _____ summer _____

9. _____ shoes _____

10. _____ fright _____

Ask yourself what each modifier tells about its subject. Does it tell who, where, when, how, why, which, or what? Also, review each of your examples to be sure you still have only a subject plus one or two modifiers, and not a subject-plus-predicate structure.

3 The Simple Predicate

The predicate verb gives information about what a subject does or what a subject is. When a verb tells us what a subject does, it is called an "action" verb. Verbs that tell us what a subject is are called "linking" verbs. These verbs, such as "is," "was," and "seems," have very little action in them. They give information about a subject's present, past, or future condition.

Verb tenses

The predicate verb includes information about when an action is complete. We begin with three basic tenses: the present, the past, and the future. The following list shows a group of action verbs and the forms they take in these three tenses. The subject is the pronoun "I."

	Present	*Past*	*Future*
1. I	strike	struck	will strike
2. I	hit	hit	will hit
3. I	see	saw	will see
4. I	follow	followed	will follow
5. I	work	worked	will work
6. I	presume	presumed	will presume
7. I	sing	sang	will sing
8. I	qualify	qualified	will qualify
9. I	assume	assumed	will assume
10. I	observe	observed	will observe

The "regular" form for the past tense, when the subject is "I," has "-d" or "-ed" at the end. Many verbs, like "strike" and "see," are "irregular," and take a special form for the past tense. Dictionaries give information about the proper past tense forms of irregular verbs. If you are in doubt, be sure to check the dictionary.

Using "I" as your subject, fill in the blanks with the correct present, past, or future forms of the verbs below.

	Present	*Past*	*Future*
1. I	_____	sat	_____
2. I	eat	_____	_____
3. I	_____	_____	will object

	Present	*Past*	*Future*
4. I	find	_____	_____
5. I	_____	_____	will show
6. I	have	_____	_____
7. I	contain	_____	_____
8. I	let	_____	_____
9. I	_____	fought	_____
10. I	_____	practiced	_____

Helper verbs: perfect tenses

The examples above show that the future tense needs a helper verb, "will," to express a future idea. Other helper verbs make it possible to express yet different tenses. The perfect tenses express different past tense relationships than the simple past tenses above. They use helper verbs with the past participle of the main verb. Dictionaries usually supply the past participle form for most verbs. Consider the following examples:

present perfect: I have qualified
past perfect: I had qualified
future perfect: I will have qualified

The first expression, "I have qualified," suggests that the action was done sometime in the past and need not be repeated. The second expression, "I had qualified," suggests that the action was done in the very distant past. The last expression, "I will have qualified," suggests that the action will occur in the distant future, after another action is completed. The future perfect can be a useful tense, but it is not used as much as it once was. Therefore, in the following examples, provide the present perfect and past perfect forms of the verbs listed. Use "I" as your subject.

	Present	*Present perfect*	*Past perfect*
1. I	eat	have eaten	had eaten
2. I	saw	have seen	had seen
3. I	met	have met	had met

4. I	fight	have fought	had fought
5. I	let	have let	had let
6. I	explain	have explained	had explained
7. I	possess	_____	_____
8. I	suppose	_____	_____
9. I	maintain	_____	_____
10. I	support	_____	_____
11. I	think	_____	_____
12. I	wink	_____	_____
13. I	sing	_____	_____
14. I	forget	_____	_____
15. I	take	_____	_____

▶ PAST PARTICIPLE POINTER

The irregular verbs in examples 1, 2, 4, and 5 have slightly different past participles than the regular verbs. But all the perfect tenses use the past participle to form their tense. "Eaten," "seen," "let," and "explained," like all the forms used in the perfect tenses above, are past participles. In the examples you are to fill in, be careful of verbs like "think," "sing," and "take." If you are in doubt of the past participle form, consult the dictionary.

Helper verbs: imperfect tenses

The imperfect tenses are used to express an ongoing action that continues. Instead of using the past participle, the imperfect tenses use the present participle, the "-ing" form. Examine the following examples; each expresses action, but it is action that continues or continued. Three tenses are involved: the present, past, and future imperfect. All need helper verbs, all use the "-ing" form of the participle.

Present imperfect	Past imperfect	Future imperfect
I am eating	I was eating	I will be eating
I am seeing	I was seeing	I will be seeing
I am following	I was following	I will be following

Fortunately, these forms are simpler than most because they are regular verbs. Consider the examples below, which use different subjects than "I."

Present imperfect	Past imperfect	Future imperfect
We are laughing	They were laughing	He will be laughing
You are sitting	We were sitting	They will be sitting
She is singing	You were singing	We will be singing

Fill in the spaces below with verbs of your own choosing. Supply the proper helper verbs in each instance.

Present imperfect	Past imperfect	Future imperfect
1. I _____	You were boasting	We _____
2. Everyone is fighting	She _____	They _____
3. He _____	Fred was winking	Our friends _____
4. Carlos _____	Leila _____	You folks will be waiting
5. Toniette is smiling	We _____	Nobody _____

▶ **PRESENT PARTICIPLE POINTER**

In order to qualify as a predicate verb, every present participle must have a helper verb. Leaving out the helper verb is one of the most common mistakes in writing. All sentences must have a predicate verb in order to be complete. Were you to leave out the helper verb in any of the examples or exercises above, you would not have a complete predicate. "You were boasting" is a subject plus a predicate verb. The predicate verb is "were boasting." The expression: "You boasting" has no predicate verb. All it has is the subject plus the present participle. When you edit your own work, be sure that you have not omitted any helper verbs from the present participles. Go back now to see that you have not left any helper verbs out of the exercise above.

Subject plus the simple predicate

We are now ready to construct the basic sentence:

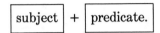

subject + predicate.

Notice that the use of helper verbs depends on the tense of the verb. Remember that helper verbs are always used with present participles. Examine the examples, then supply your own in the spaces available. Use the verb forms provided and experiment with as many tenses as possible.

Verb form	*Subject*	*Predicate*
1. halt	Carlos	halted.
2. wink	Mother	was winking.
3. read	Jasper	will be reading.
4. laugh	All of us	were laughing.
5. eat	The coach	has eaten.
6. hit	Reggie	will be hitting.
7. fly	Marjy	was flying.
8. cough	Inez or Rita	is coughing.
9. explain	Alicia	had explained.
10. insist	The officer	insisted.
11. sulk	My friend	_____ .
12. admit	Fred and I	_____ .
13. supervise	Jasper	_____ .
14. draw	The artist	_____ .
15. remember	You	_____ .
16. compose	Somebody else	_____ .

Verb form	Subject	Predicate
17. recoil	My uncle	_____ .
18. stop	The clock	_____ .
19. tour	The busload	_____ .
20. win	Our team	_____ .
21. cook	The chef	_____ .
22. vote	The senior class	_____ .
23. protect	Lydia	_____ .
24. film	The crew	_____ .
25. smoke	Even Rita	_____ .

As a way of double-checking your knowledge of the predicate verb, fill in the spaces after the ten examples below using any subject + predicate structure you wish. Try, as you did above, to represent as many different tenses as possible. In addition to the helper verbs you used above, try using some of these:

1. is	8. should be	15. should have been
2. was	9. could be	16. will have been
3. am	10. would be	17. must have been
4. are	11. can not be	18. could have been
5. were	12. had been	19. used to be
6. will be	13. have been	20. has been
7. might be	14. might have been	21. would have been

1. Scooter should be filming today.
2. He has been nominated for an award.
3. I could have been starring in that picture.
4. Jasper must have been pleased about it.
5. He might have been left out.

6. Instead, he <u>might be helping</u> with the cameras.
7. He <u>has been known</u> as a photographer.
8. His camera style <u>can not be faulted</u>.
9. We <u>might have been working</u> together on this film.
10. But I <u>have been chosen</u> for a CBS Special.

Study the examples above very carefully. Note they follow the pattern: subject + helper verbs + present or past participle. The entire predicate verb structure is underlined. In your examples, do the same. Also, try to connect your sentences by making them relate to each other as in the examples, which narrate a story.

1. _____

2. _____

3. _____

4. _____

5. _____

6. _____

7. _____

8. _____

9. _____

10. _____

4 The Predicate with Adverb Modifiers

Sometimes a simple predicate can easily stand alone, as in the exercises in Unit 3. But more often, we add modifiers to the predicate to give us information about *when*, *where*, and *how* the predicate action is done. One way of writing fuller and better sentences is to insist on completing the predicate with adverbs that give information to answer these questions:

> When?
> Where?
> How?
> Why?
> What are the conditions?

The predicate with adverbs relating to time

We begin with a basic kind of information: time. We want to know the "when" of the predicate. Most of the following examples are from the exercise in Unit 3 on page 13. The adverb modifiers are underlined.

1. Mother was winking all the time.
2. Jasper will usually be reading.
3. Marjy was never flying.
4. Inez or Rita is coughing right now.
5. Carlos halted afterward.

Notice in the next examples, the adverbs do not come immediately before or immediately after the verb. They are still modifying the predicate and telling us about the "time when" something is done.

6. Sooner or later, we will be satisfied.
7. Until now, Jimmie-John was leaving.
8. Instantly, the police officer swung around.
9. Soon, we all will be driving.
10. Last night, the whole group assembled early.

Some more adverbs that tell about time are: after, first, last, next, this time, always, ever again, immediately, long ago, before, then, today. In the following exercise, use as many of those listed above and as many new adverbs as possible. Look for new ways to modify the predicate.

1. Jasper writes _____.

2. My favorite cousin could speak _____.

3. _____ we can have luncheon.

4. Sullivan's girlfriend may never swim _____.

5. _____ Carlos will try again.

6. _____ the Model Congress began.

7. The President of Tanzania was cheered _____.

8. _____ nobody will say anything.

9. They were all speaking _____.

10. _____ we met their friends.

The predicate with adverbs relating to place

The principle of adverb modifiers of place is the same as that for adverb modifiers of time. Even the punctuation pattern, explained in the Pointer above, is the same. We use a wide variety of adverbs of place, such as: next door, here, there, beyond, outside, right, left, up, down, inside, near, far, away, behind, beneath, above, in, out, and many more. The following examples use the same principles discussed earlier.

1. My friend was talking nearby.
2. Outside, Jimmie was hiding.
3. A few steps to the left, Rita was dancing alone.
4. Lisa was waiting nearby.
5. Linc was laughing around the corner.

Provide your own adverbs of place below.

1. Jimmie-John wanted a seat _____ his teacher.

2. _____ my friend found a quarter.

3. Alma Perado would not do her dance _____.

4. They were running _____.

5. The solidarity meeting was held _____.

6. The grandstand was _____ from campus.

The predicate with adverbs relating to manner

Just as adverbs tell us when and where something happens, they can tell us how it happens. Perhaps such adverbs are even more common than those of place and time. We cannot list all the adverbs that tell us how something is done, but some of the more important ones are: slowly, sharply, fast, loud, soft, dull, better, worse, stupidly, cunningly, gracefully, miserably, happily, brightly, jovially, loosely, clumsily, expertly, softly. The list is almost endless, particularly if we add expressions such as: like an expert, against our better judgment, with a sly smile, and so on. The examples below concentrate on the basic approach to using adverbs of manner to complete the predicate.

1. Winniette was working <u>steadily</u>.
2. Reggie Jackson could be hitting <u>better</u>.
3. <u>Slowly and painfully</u>, the last runner came home.
4. The television set shone <u>brightly</u>.

Provide your own adverbs of manner in the exercises below using some of the adverbs of manner listed above and adding adverbs of manner of your own. Aim for variety and try to make your sentences as interesting as you can.

1. Sara Beth walked off the job _____.

2. Some of us trembled _____.

3. The boss _____ told her off.

4. Everyone in the place protested _____.

5. Even Rita argued _____ for her.

6. _____ the boss admitted he might be wrong.

7. After a while, Sara Beth _____ came back.

8. The boss complained _____ than before.

9. Then Jasper's explanation was offered _____.

10. Now Sara Beth performs her job _____.

The following sentences need adverb modifiers to make their predicates fuller and more meaningful. You decide whether to use modifiers of time, place, or manner. Try to find original modifiers that will help make these sentences lively and interesting. Be prepared to identify your adverbs according to their function.

1. Jasper wanted Rita to run for President of the Council _____.

2. _____ Rita wouldn't hear of it.

3. But then Inez and Luella mentioned it to her _____.

4. The outgoing president spoke to her _____.

5. _____ Rita decided to consider it.

6. Jasper learned of Rita's decision _____.

7. _____ Jasper knew he could handle the campaign

_____.

8. _____ Rita told Cici and Deanne.

9. They reacted _____.

10. _____ the election cannot occur _____.

5   The Predicate with Objects and Complements

Action verbs

Predicate verbs are of two types. The first is an action, or transitive, verb, a verb that takes an object. In this type of predicate, the verb does something to an object. In the examples immediately following, the action verb is underlined and the object is boxed (adverb modifiers begin or end some sentences):

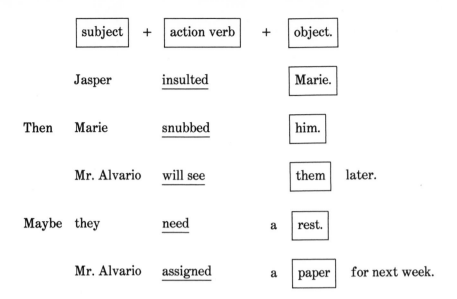

subject	+	action verb	+	object.
Jasper		insulted		Marie.
Then Marie		snubbed		him.
Mr. Alvario		will see		them later.
Maybe they		need	a	rest.
Mr. Alvario		assigned	a	paper for next week.

In these examples, the subject expresses action through the predicate verb, which carries that action on to another noun, the object. The object, like the subject, can be a proper noun, "Marie"; a common noun, "paper"; or an abstract idea, "rest." It can also be a pronoun, such as him or her. In other words, an object is very much like a subject in that it is a noun; but it is unlike a subject in that instead of doing the action, the action is done to it.

In the following sentences the action verbs are underlined and their objects are boxed. All the objects are relatively simple. Later, as you will discover in our work with infinitives and gerunds, the objects can be very complicated. But until we reach that point, be sure to keep your own objects as straightforward as the examples below.

1. Mr. Alvario could not hear Jasper at all.

2. No one knew the answer to the question.

3. Before long, Sofie drew a diagram on the board.

4. Next to the diagram she put several symbols.

5. The symbols meant nothing to any of us.

6. In all probability, Sofie was actually kidding us.

7. She <u>had diagramed</u> Snoopy's $\boxed{\text{doghouse.}}$

8. The symbols <u>spelled</u> $\boxed{\text{"Linus."}}$

9. Mr. Alvario and Sofie <u>were teasing</u> the whole $\boxed{\text{class.}}$

In the five sentences that follow, underline the predicate verb. Then, box the object. Remember that the object receives the action of the verb; it is the thing to which something is done. In some cases, the action of the verb may be as strong as the action in "kick." In other cases it may be as faint as the action in "sleep." You may have to study some of these sentences carefully to establish just what the action in them is.

1. The promoters of the tennis tournament imagined a sellout.

2. Unfortunately, the crowds never could get the tickets.

3. The printing machine ruined them.

4. The promoters never expected that.

5. The day of the tournament, however, the players let the crowds in for nothing.

Provide your own objects in the following sentences:

1. Mr. Alvario teaches _____ .

2. After school, the guys go down and play a little _____ .

3. When Mr. Alvario sees _____ , he gives him

_____ .

4. Naturally, Jasper can't tell him a _____ .

5. So he explains the _____ as best he can.

In the following spaces, provide your own sentences. Underline the predicate verb and box the object. Try to make your sentences form a paragraph, as in the examples above. Tell about a familiar activity you took part in recently.

1. _____

2. _____

3. _____

4. _____

5. _____

Linking verbs

The other kind of predicate verb, the linking, or intransitive, verb, does not express action. Instead, it links the subject with the complement. There are two types of complements: the noun complement, which restates the subject; and the adjective complement, which describes the subject. In the following examples, the linking verb is underlined and the noun complement is boxed.

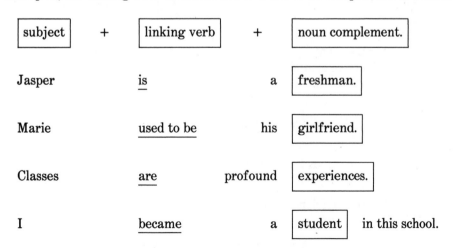

subject	+	linking verb	+	noun complement.

Jasper   <u>is</u>   a   freshman.

Marie   <u>used to be</u>   his   girlfriend.

Classes   <u>are</u>   profound   experiences.

I   <u>became</u>   a   student   in this school.

In these examples, the noun complement basically restates the subject.

The adjective complement works in the same way. The model for using the adjective complement is:

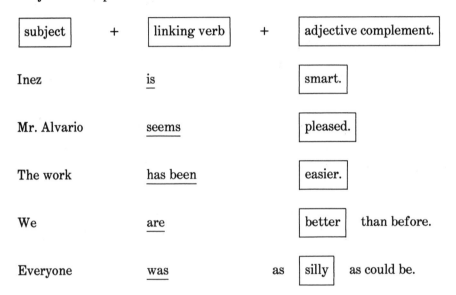

subject + linking verb + adjective complement.

Inez is smart.

Mr. Alvario seems pleased.

The work has been easier.

We are better than before.

Everyone was as silly as could be.

In the examples that follow, five sentences use the noun complement and five use the adjective complement. In the space provided, put NC or AC, as a way of identifying each.

_____ 1. My friend was very tall.

_____ 2. Sometimes he became embarrassed.

_____ 3. His girlfriend was not exactly a midget.

_____ 4. But she was so short he could eat spaghetti off her head.

_____ 5. Today my friend is <u>a basketball center</u>.

_____ 6. By playing basketball, he has become <u>confident</u>.

_____ 7. His girlfriend is <u>a gourmet cook</u> these days.

_____ 8. She is not <u>afraid</u> to be seen at his side.

_____ 9. They say she expects to become <u>a professional chef</u>.

_____ 10. Her specialty is <u>lasagna</u>.

In the following examples, there is a space after each sentence for you to put in your own noun complements or adjective complements. Aim for variety. Identify the complements by writing NC or AC in the space provided before each sentence.

_____ 1. Inez, when she is alone, is _____.

_____ 2. People who act stuck up are _____.

_____ 3. We aren't stuck up, we're _____.

_____ 4. But when we get mad, we become _____.

_____ 5. Luckily, we stay _____ most of the time.

_____ 6. If we appear _____, it's because you don't know us.

_____ 7. After a while, we become _____, or so they say.

_____ 8. Of course, Inez says we're _____.

_____ 9. She isn't _____ because she doesn't see us much.

_____ 10. You just can't be _____ about people you don't know.

▶ **POINTER**

When you have finished the exercise above, go over it to be sure you have not used an "-ing" form of the verb to complete any of the assignment. For instance, if in number 1 you said, "Inez when she is alone, is smoking," you did not provide a complement. What you provided was part of a predicate verb. "Is smoking," "is sleeping," "is standing," "is running" are all verbs in the present perfect tense. If you said, "Inez is happy" or "Inez is our new president," you provided an adjective complement and a noun complement, respectively. Examine each of your examples to be sure you did not provide a verb in the present perfect tense.

Just to be sure that your command of objects, noun complements, and adjective complements is complete, write five sentences in the spaces provided. Underline the complement and identify it in the space before each sentence. Make the sentences relate to one another as if they were part of a story or part of a paragraph and try to make them as interesting as possible.

_____ 1. _____

_____ 2. _____

_____ 3. _____

_____ 4. _____

_____ 5. _____

6 The Independent Clause

Every complete sentence must have at least two basic parts: a subject and a predicate verb. The ⬚subject + ⬚predicate structure, or pattern, is basic to English speech.

This structure is also called an independent clause because it can stand alone and can make a complete statement. These qualities distinguish it from the subordinate clause, which also has a subject and a predicate, but begins with a subordinating word such as "before," "because," "although," or "until." Because the subordinating word raises a question, such as "who?" "where?" "when?" "why?" or "how?" it makes the subordinate clause depend for its full meaning on another part of the sentence. The independent clause is that other part, and without it no sentence is complete.

Since the independent clause is the basic unit for making a meaningful statement in the English language, you must be able to recognize it in your writing. Each sentence you write must contain at least one independent clause; otherwise, it is *not* a complete sentence. It will not make a complete statement, and will only confuse or annoy your reader. Remember: the independent clause always has a subject and a predicate and makes a complete statement. Often, an independent clause has modifiers added to the subject and or to the predicate, but it does not need to have them to be complete in its meaning.

You can develop a good sense of what an independent clause is and what it looks like by studying the examples that follow. All these independent clauses have their subjects and predicates underlined and identified: S for subject; P for predicate. Read the sentences aloud to reinforce the way independent clauses sound.

1. The <u>man</u> in the tattered clothes <u>slashed</u> at the rope with his machete.
      S   P

2. <u>Yolande</u> <u>screamed</u> bloody murder.
      S   P

3. <u>He</u> <u>was</u> obviously in danger.
     S P

4. The <u>rope</u> <u>tied</u> him to a huge tree.
      S   P

5. An immense green and black <u>snake</u> <u>was slithering</u> toward him.
                           S   P

6. <u>Yolande</u> <u>seized</u> the machete.
    S   P

7. <u>She</u> <u>raised</u> it high over her head with both hands.
   S   P

8. The glistening <u>machete</u> <u>swung</u> down on the writhing snake.
              S   P

9. The frightened <u>man</u> <u>gave</u> her a look of heartfelt gratitude.
          S   P

10. Immediately, <u>Yolande</u> <u>began</u> to help him break free.
           S   P

All these examples are like the complete sentences you have seen in earlier exercises. All they may lack are extra modifiers to add information or to clarify their meaning. Use the following checklist to decide if a structure is an independent clause.

        1. Does it have a subject?
        2. Does it have a verb that can be a predicate?
        3. Does it make a complete statement?

Remember: if a clause begins with a word that makes it depend for its meaning on something else, such as the answer to the questions "Who?" "Where?" "When?" "Why?" or "How?" it does not express a complete idea, and it is not an independent clause.

The following list has some independent clauses and some structures that are not independent clauses. As a check, underline the subject and the predicate. For examples that are not independent clauses, indicate what is wrong: no subject (NS); no predicate verb (NP); a word at the beginning that makes it a subordinate clause (SC).

_____ 1. When you live in the city.

_____ 2. You can travel by subway or by bus.

_____ 3. Most people, knowing the rush hours on the subway.

_____ 4. They travel at a different time of day.

_____ 5. People often must travel during the rush hour.

_____ 6. Because they have places to go.

_____ 7. When the train pulls up to the waiting crowd.

_____ 8. Little children search for their lost parents.

_____ 9. Busy workers rushing off in all directions on their homeward journey.

_____ 10. Confusion and haste.

A quick review of what you did in the previous parts of this unit will help if you had trouble with the examples above.

Spaces are provided below for you to write your own independent clauses. Follow the pattern of ⌐subject¬ + ⌐predicate¬, underline each of them, and write S or P under them for identification. Check each of your sentences carefully, using the checklist provided for the previous exercises.

1. _____

2. _____

3. _____

4. _____

5. _____

6. _____

7. _____

8. _____

9. _____

10. _____

7 The Sentence Fragment

One of the criticisms many writers receive is that they do not always write complete sentences. Instead, they sometimes write fragments. A fragment is only part of a sentence. It can be a subject or a predicate each standing alone, or it can be a subject + predicate structure that is not really a completed statement.

First we will concentrate on recognizing sentence fragments. It is essential to recognize fragments so that you can learn how to edit them out of your work. Once you recognize them, fragments can be changed into complete sentences.

Fragments with no verbs

A fragment with no verb will usually have a subject and some of the adverb phrases that belong with the missing predicate verb. A simple, but typical, example follows:

> Mr. Alvario in front of the blackboard.

We have a subject, "Mr. Alvario"; we have an adverb phrase of place, "in front of the blackboard"; but we have no predicate verb. What is Mr. Alvario *doing* in front of the blackboard? We ask this question in vain since the writer has not told us what Mr. Alvario is doing. To make this a sentence we must add a verb. The following revision, with the verb underlined, is now a complete sentence:

> Mr. Alvario was standing in front of the blackboard.

Often, verbs of being are left out of sentences because it is clear to the writer that direct action is not implied. Instead, a simple state of being is implied. Consider these examples:

> We with you all the way.
> Nobody from down home but me.
> Rudy and Hilda in love since childhood.

In each case a form of the verb "to be" is needed. Note the fragments that are now converted into sentences. The verbs are underlined:

> We are with you all the way.

> Nobody is from down home but me.

> Rudy and Hilda have been in love since childhood.

Decide which of the ten examples that follow are fragments. For each fragment, provide a workable verb in the space provided. Then indicate with an X just where you would place that verb in order to make the fragment a complete sentence. In sentences that are already complete, underline the subject and box the verb.

1. Women from all over America. _____

2. They together in a mass conference in Washington. _____

3. Women were speaking out on the question of equal rights. _____

4. But it not the first time for such a gathering. _____

5. Many gatherings like this over the last decade and a half. _____

6. Now an amendment to the U.S. Constitution the issue. _____

7. The question about men and women being equal in the eyes of the law.

_____

8. Equality may have to wait until later. _____

Go over your work and ask your instructor to make up some more examples for you if you did not get at least half of these sentences right. Do the same for the other exercises in this unit.

Fragments with verbs not used as predicate verbs

It is more difficult to identify a fragment when it has a verb as well as a subject. The problem occurs with a verb that is part of a subordinate clause instead of being the verb for the independent clause. The way to identify such fragments is to find the subject of the sentence, and then to determine whether it has its own predicate verb. We can see this more clearly if we take the first example we used and modify it slightly:

> Mr. Alvario in front of the blackboard while everyone waited
> for the bell at the end of class.

The situation is much as it was in the original example except that an addition has been made, giving information about what "everyone" was doing. "While" is an adverb introducing a subordinate clause telling about "everyone." "Everyone" is a new subject, and "waited" is its verb. Mr. Alvario is still not *doing* anything. We must still insert a verb, such as "was standing," after "Mr. Alvario" if we are to create a complete sentence.

The following examples will show that such fragments are not always easy to identify. In the first five examples below, the subject of the main clause is underlined for clarity. Each example includes a subordinate clause with its own subject and predicate verb. All these examples are fragments because the subject of the independent clause is lacking a predicate verb.

1. My friend from a place where everyone dances.
2. Even Tony, who doesn't like music.
3. Rita, Inez, and Judy when the band plays a good rock tune.
4. Some good dance tunes for people who like slow romantic dancing.
5. Of course Elton John good for when you want to do an energetic dance.

These can all be made into satisfactory sentences by including a predicate verb for the subject of the independent clause. The following sentences, with their predicate verbs supplied in the independent clauses, offer one way of converting fragments.

1. My friend comes from a place where everyone dances.
2. Even Tony, who doesn't like music, dances.
3. Rita, Inez, and Judy dance when the band plays a good rock tune.
4. Some good dance tunes exist for people who like slow romantic dancing.
5. Of course Elton John is good for when you want to do an energetic dance.

The following examples are either fragments or sentences. On the line after a fragment, write a verb that will make the fragment a sentence. Then place an X where this verb should go in the fragment. On the line after a sentence, copy the verb from the sentence.

1. Rita the woman who wanted to be a lawyer when she started college.

   _____

2. The question what you want to be in high school. _____

3. They our old family friends, such as those who knew my dad.

   _____

4. Too many suggestions from people who thought they knew what I
   should do. _____

5. They wrong, even if they meant well. _____

6. They told me, nursing the thing for me._____

7. Actually, though they convinced me at first, I did not really want a
   career in nursing. _____

8. Nursing very good, even though I can't stand sick people. _____

9. When I'm with sick people, I sick too. _____

10. Fortunately Rita knew right away, but I confused more and more about
    what to do. _____

11. Counselors at the school when I was looking for ideas. _____

12. My profile based on the courses I like to take. _____

13. It gave me a surprising picture of what my skills were. _____

14. The profile that I might make a good accountant or even a banker.

    _____

15. If nursing might make me sick, banking me rich? _____

Fragments with "-ing," "-ed," "-en" verb forms but no predicate verbs

Fragments most commonly occur when a participle is used in place of the predicate verb. (See Section I, Unit 3 for present and past participle pointers.) The present participle, the form ending with "-ing," is the one usually used, so we will concentrate most on it. Here is a typical fragment with a present participle in place of the predicate verb:

Reggie Jackson hitting a home run while I was out of the room.

In this fragment we get a sense of what the writer wished to say, but everything is not clear. We sense that the action is not yet complete because the participle needs a helper verb to make it state a completed action. The helper is underlined in the next example, which is now a complete sentence.

Reggie Jackson <u>was</u> hitting a home run while I was out of the room.

Often the past participle will give the same kind of trouble as the present participle. For instance, the word "televised" in the next example is not a predicate verb. It is incomplete and needs a helper verb to make it function in the independent clause as a genuine verb.

The office party held when I should be back in school.

The correct form for this, with the entire predicate verb underlined, is:

The office party <u>will be held</u> when I should be back in school.

In the following examples, supply the helper verb needed to make the participle a predicate verb. Write the helper verb in the space provided and place an X where the verb should go in the sentence. A few examples are complete sentences, but most of them are fragments. For the sentences that are already complete, put a check mark in the space. Before you do the following exercises, it may help to review the verb forms for the imperfect and perfect tenses on pages 10–13.

1. My friend Jake having a lot of trouble with used cars. _____

2. Because he didn't have much money, Jake spending a lot on repairs.

_____

3. Jake buying a few dogs, and even repairs couldn't keep them going.

_____

4. Jake stunned by the way little cars seemed to burn valves. _____

5. Big cars burnt a lot of gas and ruining mufflers all the time. _____

6. Jake stuck by the side of the road often these days. _____

7. Friends talking to him about picking up a new mid-sized car.

   _____

8. But he's been convinced that taking out a loan will be even worse than

   keeping his old car going. _____

9. Jake convinced there is no way to beat the automotive industry.

   _____

10. It is tough, but Jake eyeing a good used bicycle the other day.

    _____

11. Obviously he caught up in the endless cycle of repairs. _____

12. With his kind of luck, even a bike cost him a bundle if he is not careful.

    _____

13. Someone mentioned a horse to him just last weekend. _____

14. He checked on the cost of oats, and it is going up. _____

15. Marceau trying to unload an Edsel and thought he would give Jake a

    call. _____

8 The Run-On Sentence

A fragment is not enough of a structure to be a sentence, but a run-on
sentence is too much of a structure for a single sentence to bear. The run-on
sentence does not end when it should. Usually two or more sentences are
joined together with no punctuation. Here is an example:

We were mad at Fred he kept us waiting all day.

The simplest correction is to end the first sentence with a period and begin the second with a capital letter:

We were mad at Fred. He kept us waiting all day.

Another version of this problem is the comma splice. It is basically the same as the example above, but there is a comma where the period ought to be. The comma splice is very difficult to correct because the writer usually feels the comma has solved the problem of pausing between sentences. The writer does not realize that the problem occurred because there are two sentences involved. An example, with its corrected version, follows:

Marvin wanted to be a chef, after college he went to cooking school.

Marvin wanted to be a chef. After college he went to cooking school.

The following examples are all run-on sentences. Read them carefully and correct each sentence on the lines provided.

1. Jenny Foster was an adventurous woman after she got her automobile license she wanted to learn to fly.

_____

_____

_____

2. Jenny spent a good deal of her free time at the local airport under different circumstances she might have tried a big city field.

_____

_____

_____

3. The local field was really pretty good for her, she got to work out on Cessnas and a friend's Cheyenne.

_____

_____

_____

4. Billy Hitchcock, the Second World War ace, took a look at her one day, she was a natural flyer, he realized soon enough.

_____

_____

_____

5. He took a liking to her before she knew it she was doing stunts on his modified Mustang, a vintage plane she just loved to fly.

_____

_____

_____

_____

▶ PUNCTUATION POINTER
The Semicolon

Actually, all the examples above represent bad punctuation. One of the ways to correct the problem is to make separate sentences of the parts. But there is another way that some writers prefer. Use the semicolon (;) between sentences. The semicolon has the force of a period, but it also lets the writer join two thoughts closer together than they would be if they were in separate sentences. All the sentences above could legitimately use the semicolon in this way:

Some people enjoy tennis; others seem to like golf.

Either solution is good, you may feel free to choose either one.

Overloaded sentences

Run-on sentences are created usually because the writer sees a close connection between two sentences. The failure to punctuate correctly makes the relationship unclear. Sometimes the failure is caused by accident. Sometimes it is caused by the writer's not realizing the need to relate the sentences to one another.

Many run-on sentences are not caused by problems of punctuation. They result from trying to cram too much information into one sentence. This produces the overloaded sentence. The way to fix such a sentence is to examine it carefully to see that all the subordinate clauses and phrases are clearly connected to the independent clause at the heart of the sentence. See Section II, "Principles of Subordination," for a complete discussion of clauses and phrases. The examples below are taken from student essays. They show some typical problems shared by many writers.

> As the story progresses all the things that Okonkwo had worked so hard for started to dissolve, at first on account of his own *chi*, or god, and later because of the coming of the white man.

The problem with this sentence arises at the first comma. The writer actually has a complete sentence by the time he reaches the comma, so all the remaining phrases are the overload. Technically, the phrases after the comma should be clauses. They should be attached with coordinate conjunctions (see Section III, "Prinicples of Coordination"). Or, they should be separated and made into a new sentence. Probably the easiest way of rewriting this sentence would be:

> As the story progresses, all the things that Okonkwo had worked so hard for started to dissolve. At first they dissolved on account of his own *chi*, or god, and later because of the coming of the white man.

The elements added to the original are a comma after "progresses"; a period after "dissolve"; a capital letter for "At"; and a subject + predicate, "they dissolved," for the second sentence. The most important thing to remember about this way of solving the problem is that the overload will almost always come in the second half of the sentence. Once you realize it is an overload, you can remedy the situation by making the overload a separate sentence.

The next example is slightly different, but the solution that follows it is basically the same as that above.

> I would have written about the friends I have met but I only know a few by name the rest by room number.

> I would have written about the friends I have met, but I only know a few by name. The rest I know by room number.

The following examples are all drawn from actual essays. Study them carefully and rewrite them in order to avoid the run-on sentence.

1. In a society where a man's status is judged by his strength and bravery, and how a man takes care of his household Unoka would not do his harvesting until the last moment he was too busy drinking palm wine and playing the flute.

_____

_____

_____

_____

_____

2. Fred appears in another situation where he is seen in a market, there a customer takes for granted that he is one of the employees.

_____

_____

_____

_____

3. Fred was accused of a crime that he did not commit because Fred happened to be black and around at the time, he was picked up by the police, beaten and forced to sign a confession that he was not allowed to read.

_____

_____

_____

_____

_____

_____

4. He felt that he would not be noticeable to people, because he had stayed in that cave and he had forgotten about people this was while he thought the man did not see him.

_____

_____

_____

_____

5. After a dream has been put off it does not just shrink up and fade away, it isn't thought of and then rubbed out like a sore, it has no odor of anything rotten, but it doesn't have sweetness either, it's just there.

_____

_____

_____

_____

_____

_____

6. He keeps moving off a little further and further and the pitcher throws the ball and he is off it is all up to him now no one else.

_____

_____

_____

_____

_____

7. By having this crash, Todd found himself, this is where the story's title "Flying Home" comes in.

_____

_____

_____

_____

Correcting someone else's writing can be very helpful, but it is probably even more helpful to correct your own work. Go through some of your recent writing and find examples of run-on or overloaded sentences. Write each one in the first space provided, then write your revision of the sentence. Be prepared to talk about the ways in which you made your revision.

Your run-on sentence: _____

_____

_____

_____

Your revision: _____

_____

_____

_____

Your run-on sentence: _____

_____

_____

_____

Your revision: _____

_____

_____

_____

Your run-on sentence: _____

_____

_____

_____

Your revision: _____

_____

_____

_____

9   Subject and Predicate Agreement

A subject that refers to one thing or idea must be matched with a predicate verb that also refers to one thing or idea. A subject that refers to more than one thing or idea must be matched with a predicate verb that also refers to more than one thing or idea. In other words, a singular subject must have a singular verb, and a plural subject must have a plural verb. The fact that a great many writers do not always make the subject and the verb agree is probably due to three problems. The first is carelessness—the writer has changed in mid-sentence from singular to plural, or vice versa. Or, second, the writer may not recognize the singular or plural forms of either the subject or the verb. A third possibility is that the writer's dialect may not pronounce the standard verb ending. In the first case, rereading carefully —or proofreading—is essential. In the second and third cases, some of the material below can be of help.

Identifying singular and plural subjects

The most common rule for making a subject plural is to add an "-s," "-es," or "-ies" to the end of the subject. In some cases (numbers 7 and 9), the final letter must be dropped when forming the plural. Some examples of making singular subjects plural follow.

Singular subject	*Subject made plural*
1. market	1. markets
2. governess	2. governesses
3. grass	3. grasses
4. nest	4. nests
5. explosion	5. explosions
6. nuance	6. nuances
7. vacancy	7. vacancies

8. disturbance	8. disturbances
9. spy	9. spies
10. clause	10. clauses

Some writers may have trouble forming plurals of words because, in their everyday speech, they do not pronounce the "s" sound. Visual double-checking, particularly if you have been told about such a problem, will help avoid leaving off the plural "s." However, some words do not follow the standard pattern. They have a special way of forming the plural. Among the most common of these words are:

Singular subject	Subject made plural
1. phenomenon	1. phenomena
2. datum	2. data
3. foot	3. feet
4. tooth	4. teeth
5. goose	5. geese
6. louse	6. lice
7. child	7. children
8. man	8. men
9. sheep	9. sheep
10. crisis	10. crises

Some words are troublesome because they sound as if they are plural because they end in "s" or an "s" sound. Some examples of such words are: box, silence, importance, sense, diligence, distance, climax. If you are in doubt about words like these, consult a dictionary. It will tell you whether the form of the word you want to use is singular or plural.

Some words have a plural ending, although they are singular in meaning. These are often quite difficult and must be learned separately. Some examples of these words are: politics, economics, mathematics, measles, physics.

In the following list, decide whether the form of the subject is singular or plural. Then provide the other form of the subject, singular or plural as needed.

Subject	Singular	Plural	Supply the other form
1. priority	_____	_____	_____
2. Chinese	_____	_____	_____
3. women	_____	_____	_____
4. finder	_____	_____	_____
5. data	_____	_____	_____

Subject	Singular	Plural	Supply the other form
6. pies	_____	_____	_____
7. stimuli	_____	_____	_____
8. offense	_____	_____	_____
9. kindness	_____	_____	_____
10. quantity	_____	_____	_____
11. office	_____	_____	_____
12. vice	_____	_____	_____
13. vests	_____	_____	_____
14. deer	_____	_____	_____
15. clue	_____	_____	_____

Singular and plural predicate verbs

Problems with singular or plural forms of predicate verbs usually occur in the present tense, third-person singular and plural. The rule for making the third-person (he, she, it) singular verb is the opposite of that for making a noun singular. Taking away the "s" from the verb makes it singular; adding the "s" makes the verb plural. In the following list, each verb has a third-person subject to help make the point clearer.

Third-person singular verb	Third-person plural verb
1. Mr. Alvario sends	1. the students send
2. he fights	2. they fight
3. Inez does	3. the men do
4. she teaches	4. they teach
5. Sandy eats	5. the people eat
6. nobody allows	6. we all allow
7. distance permits	7. distances permit

8. nonsense prevents	8. experiments prevent
9. it is	9. they are
10. friendship helps	10. plans help

All the verbs above are in the present tense, where most of the problems occur. In the past tense we often use the same verb form for singular and plural. The past tense forms for the verbs listed above are singular *and* plural, depending on the subject you use with them: sent, fought, did, taught, ate, allowed, permitted, prevented, and helped. The only verb omitted is number 9, "is/are." This verb is irregular, and it causes special problems. The past singular form is "was"; the past plural form is "were." To make sure we use this verb correctly, we must memorize its forms. The conjugation, in present and past tenses, of the verb "to be" is:

Present tense	*Past tense*
I am	I was
you are	you were
he, she, it is	he, she, it was
we are	we were
you are	you were
they are	they were

In the list that follows, decide whether the form of the verb supplied is singular or plural and indicate your choice on the appropriate line. Then supply the other form of the verb, singular or plural as needed.

Third-person verb	*Singular*	*Plural*	*Supply the other form*
1. visits	_____	_____	_____
2. tenses	_____	_____	_____
3. admit	_____	_____	_____
4. rectify	_____	_____	_____
5. achieve	_____	_____	_____
6. prefers	_____	_____	_____
7. militate	_____	_____	_____
8. mollify	_____	_____	_____

Third-person verb	Singular	Plural	Supply the other form
9. coordinates	_____	_____	_____
10. built	_____	_____	_____
11. frighten	_____	_____	_____
12. insist	_____	_____	_____
13. were	_____	_____	_____
14. am	_____	_____	_____
15. refurbish	_____	_____	_____

Making the subject and predicate verb agree

Now, the most important point is that the subject and the predicate verb must agree with each other. If the subject is singular, the verb must be singular; if the subject is plural, the verb must be plural. In the examples that follow the subjects and predicate verbs are in agreement. Next to each sentence indicate whether the subject and predicate verb are singular or plural.

	Singular	Plural
1. Danny Espinosa plays tennis.	_____	_____
2. His sister and brother prefer golf.	_____	_____
3. But there is no golf course nearby.	_____	_____
4. And the tennis courts are often crowded.	_____	_____
5. Sometimes they have to play paddle ball in the park.	_____	_____
6. Paddle ball is played against a concrete wall.	_____	_____

7. Naturally it is a fast and wicked game. _____ _____

8. Still, people seem to enjoy playing it. _____ _____

9. It helps Danny with his tennis. _____ _____

10. His sister and brother can have fun at
it, too. _____ _____

In the first five examples below, supply the proper form of either the subject or the predicate verb. If the verb is singular, supply a singular subject; if it is plural, supply a plural subject. Do the same for the subjects. Then, on lines 6–15, write brief sentences in which the subject and verb are in agreement. Make some subjects and verbs agree in the plural and some agree in the singular. Make every effort to have your sentences relate to each other as if they were part of a paragraph or a narrative.

	Singular	*Plural*
1. The James boys _____.	_____	_____
2. _____ wants to catch them.	_____	_____
3. _____ apparently rob banks for a living.	_____	_____
4. If they are caught, they _____.	_____	_____
5. _____ seems able to catch up to them.	_____	_____
6. _____	_____	_____
7. _____	_____	_____
8. _____	_____	_____
9. _____	_____	_____

10. _____   _____ _____

11. _____   _____ _____

12. _____   _____ _____

13. _____   _____ _____

14. _____   _____ _____

15. _____   _____ _____

10 Pronoun Agreement

Faulty pronoun agreement gives many people problems. Many pronouns refer back to the nouns (antecedents) for which they stand. In this case, both the antecedent and the pronoun must agree and be singular or plural. Often a simple editing check is enough to insure agreement. Sometimes, however, a better knowledge of pronouns and how they work is needed in order to guarantee accuracy. It is also very important to be sure that any pronoun refering back to a noun actually has that noun clearly stated for reference. When it is not clearly stated, ambiguity can make the pronoun seem weak and purposeless.

The list below includes some of the most troublesome pronouns.

Pronouns

1. that	6. its	11. their
2. this	7. some	12. one
3. who/whom	8. nobody	13. which
4. all	9. everyone	14. _____
5. any	10. each	15. _____

The blank spaces are for pronouns that you know will give you problems.

In the following examples, the pronoun is in proper agreement with its noun referent and with its verb. In each case, the word that the pronoun refers to is underlined and labeled "*ref.*"; the pronoun is underlined and labeled "*pron.*" and the verb is underlined and marked "*verb sing.*" or "*verb pl.*"

1. Pollution is a <u>problem</u> <u>that</u> <u>must be solved</u>.
   ref.   *pron.*   *verb sing.*

2. The <u>balance</u> of life <u>is</u> <u>nothing</u> to fool with.
   ref.   *verb sing.*   *pron.*

3. <u>People</u> <u>have</u> a right to <u>their</u> lives.
   ref.   *verb pl.*   *pron.*

4. <u>Lawmakers</u> <u>are</u> almost <u>all</u> in agreement.
   ref.   *verb pl.*   *pron.*

5. <u>Pollution</u> <u>is</u> <u>something</u> we cannot tolerate.
   ref.   *verb sing.*   *pron.*

6. The <u>cost</u> of cleaning up <u>is</u> <u>what</u> staggers some people.
   ref.   *verb sing.*   *pron.*

7. <u>Polluters</u> <u>think</u> of <u>themselves</u> as law-abiding people.
   ref.   *verb pl.*   *pron.*

8. In <u>California</u>, <u>which</u> <u>has</u> stiff pollution laws, cars are a hazard.
   ref.   *pron.*   *verb sing.*

9. The <u>lead</u> <u>that</u> we find in gasoline <u>is</u> a poison.
   ref.   *pron.*   *verb sing.*

10. <u>Stop pollution!</u> <u>This</u> <u>is</u> our only hope for survival.
    ref.   *pron.*   *verb sing.*

These sentences by no means represent all the problems you are likely to find in pronoun agreement, but they do include many of the most common problems. Each pronoun must refer clearly to its referent; it must agree with it in number; it must then agree with its own verb and with the verb of the referent. You may notice that some pronouns in the sentences above are not underlined: "we" in 5 and 9; "our" in 10. They do not cause the same problems as the other pronouns because they refer directly to the speaker or writer of the sentence.

In the following examples, choose a pronoun that will work in the context provided. You may choose a pronoun from the list at the beginning of this unit, or you may choose one of your own. In the first few sentences, the word to which the pronoun refers is underlined. In the remaining sentences, underline the word to which the pronoun refers to show that you recognize the referent.

1. The gymnasium now has <u>facilities</u> _____ accommodate women.

2. The <u>law</u> _____ mandated this change is called Title IX.

3. It states that now women must have <u>facilities</u> _____ are like the men's.

4. <u>Equality</u> is not _____ we can achieve overnight.

5. <u>Similarity</u> is _____ some colleges have aimed for.

6. Women have really taken advantage of _____ new accommodations.

7. Varsity sports, _____ were formerly dominated by men, now

   have _____ female counterparts.

8. Basketball, baseball, and hockey are sports _____ women now take part in.

9. These sports have _____ own fans, too.

10. In general, people find that _____ enjoy watching women play sports.

11. The change took place because women demanded _____ rights.

12. Most of _____ agree _____ the change was none too soon.

Problems with pronoun agreement are very persistent. The exercises above may be very helpful, but they may not cure the problem. Therefore, it is wise to look for examples of faulty pronoun agreement in your own writing. If you can find such examples, write them out below as you originally wrote them. Then see if you can write a corrected version in the next space.

Your original sentence: _____

_____

_____

_____

Your sentence corrected: _____

_____

_____

_____

Your original sentence: _____

_____

_____

_____

Your sentence corrected: _____

_____

_____

_____

SECTION II

Principles of Subordination

11 Subordinate Clauses: Time, Place, Action

The subordinate clause follows the pattern:

| subordinator | + | subject | + | predicate. |

But the subordinate clause is not complete in itself. By beginning with a subordinator, the writer implies that there is more to come. Subordinators are a special group of words that set the subordinate clause apart and signal that its meaning will be completed by an independent clause. The subordinators are very often the same adverb modifiers discussed in Section I, Unit 4. The model for subordinate clauses of time, place, and action is the same:

| subordinator | + | subject | + | predicate |

	subordinator	subject	predicate
Time:	When	we	went to work
Place:	Where	we	went to work
Action:	Unless	we	went to work

Each of these clauses needs something more in order for it to make sense. We want to know what happened when or where we went to work, and what will happen unless we went to work. The subordinators set up expectations of time, place, and action that must be satisfied by another clause.

One way of satisfying the expectations in each of these subordinate clauses would be to finish them this way:

> When we went to work, we were paid well.
> Where we went to work, we were paid well.
> Unless we went to work, we would not be paid at all.

You may already know it, but it is important to note that a subordinate clause can be positioned in three parts of a sentence:

1. before the main clause, as in all the examples above
2. in the middle of the main clause—
> We were, when we went to work, paid well.
3. after the main clause—
> We would not be paid well unless we went to work.

▶ **PUNCTUATION POINTER**

The rules for punctuating the subordinate clause are simple. When the subordinate clause comes first in the sentence, use a comma after

---

the subordinate clause. When the subordinate clause comes in the middle of an independent clause, use commas before and after the subordinate clause. When the subordinate clause comes after the independent clause, use no comma between the subordinate clause and the independent clause.

Subordinate clause of time

Most subordinate clauses of time will begin with a word from the following list, which you should study carefully.

Subordinators of time

1. now when
2. after
3. before
4. until
5. at a time when
6. always when

7. as soon as
8. when
9. whenever
10. while
11. eventually when
12. sometimes when

In the following list, the subordinate clauses use subordinators of time. Examine the list closely, then supply your own list of subordinate clauses of time. Try to add new subordinators of time. Be sure to write clauses that have this pattern:

| subordinator of time | + | subject | + | predicate. |

1. After we went home
2. When everyone else had left
3. Before they locked the doors
4. Until the lights went out
5. Whenever we lag behind
6. Two days after the concert
7. Now when we want to get back in
8. While the janitor is still there
9. As soon as we see him
10. Whenever the car decides to start

Your samples of subordinate clauses of time:

1. _____

2. _____

3. _____

4. _____

5. _____

Subordinate clause of place

The main subordinator of place for subordinate clauses of place is "where" and its variants.

Subordinators of place

1. where	6. close to where
2. near where	7. up to where
3. next to where	8. from wherever
4. under	9. there where
5. over	10. opposite where

The following subordinate clauses use subordinators of place. In the spaces provided after the list, supply your own subordinate clauses of place. Be sure to proofread each of your samples carefully and make sure each has this pattern:

subordinator of place + subject + predicate.

If the subject or predicate is lacking, you will have written a phrase instead of a clause.

1. In the middle where we were swimming
2. Near where they saw the waterbugs
3. Next to where Felicia almost drowned
4. Where Inez and Joselito lost a flashlight
5. Opposite the spot where Marie likes to swim
6. Under where she carved her name
7. From behind where the bullfrog sits
8. Wherever those bubbles came from
9. Over where we heard that noise
10. Behind where the hidden treasure was sunk

Your samples of subordinate clauses of place:

1. _____

2. _____

3. _____

4. _____

5. _____

► **POINTER**

Subordinate clauses beginning with "Under where she placed it," "Next to where she placed it," or similar constructions can have this kind of pattern: | preposition | + | noun clause. |

In the subordinate clauses above, "Under" and "Next to" are prepositions; the remaining words are noun clauses, objects of those prepositions. For our purposes, however, you can regard the entire structure as a subordinate clause of place, since its meaning and use are clearly supportive of our doing so.

Subordinate clause of action

Many subordinate clauses give information about the way things are done. Some give information about the causes of actions or the limits of those actions. They give information about the how, the why, and the result of actions expressed in the independent clause. It is not necessary to name every different kind of clause of action, but by examining the following list of subordinators you will see that each subordinator points toward its function, each qualifies a clause according to an action, and each sets up expectations that the independent clause will satisfy.

Subordinators of action

1. as if
2. as
3. as though
4. because
5. since
6. so that
7. in order for

8. if
9. unless
10. even
11. even though
12. although
13. while
14. whether

The following subordinate clauses use subordinators of action. In the spaces provided later, use your own subordinators of action subordinate clauses. Again, be sure each of your clauses follows the pattern for subordinate clauses:

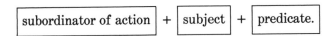

1. Unless I find my missing keys
2. Because I really need my car
3. In order that I won't miss Becky
4. Unless she gets out of the lab early
5. So that the two of us can have dinner
6. Since she expects me to be on time
7. Even though she knows I won't forget
8. Although I did forget last week
9. As if I needed this grief
10. If she is a bit later herself

Your own sample subordinate clauses of action:

1. _____

2. _____

3. _____

4. _____

5. _____

Using subordinate clauses of time, place, action in sentences

It is not enough to be able to compose subordinate clauses. Since subordinate clauses are not complete, they cannot stand as sentences. They need an independent clause to complete their meaning. The patterns for using subordinate clauses are the same, whether the clause gives information of time, place, action—or anything else. The following patterns can be used for all subordinate clauses joined with an independent clause:

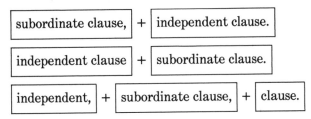

An example with subordinate clauses of time, place, and action underlined in all of these three patterns would be:

> After I figure out the way this works, I will give you a taste.
>
> I want to put a bit of this where it will do the most good.
>
> Maybe, even if you don't like ice cream, you will try this.

The following examples have the subordinate clauses underlined. In the space before the sentence, the clause is identified. Each of the examples has *both* a subordinate clause and an independent clause. Therefore, each of the examples is a complete sentence.

_____Time_____ 1. American foreign policy changed after we won the Second World War.

_____Time_____ 2. Before it was forced to enter the war, the United States was isolationist.

_____Action_____ 3. Unless American citizens were involved, the United States did not advise European politicians.

_____Action_____ 4. The United States, because it was an ocean away, felt it had little involvement in European affairs.

_____Place_____ 5. The Atlantic Ocean was the place where national interests ended.

_____Action_____ 6. Although the United States thought it was safe from harm, the events of the Second World War taught it a lesson.

_____Time_____ 7. The United States, when it took on the responsibility of defending Europe, had to become less isolated.

_____Time_____ 8. American foreign policy came of age when the Axis powers surrendered unconditionally.

_____Place_____ 9. The United States economy tried to help where the need was greatest.

<u>Action</u>   10. Europe, <u>if the United States had not awakened when it did,</u> might be under Nazi domination today.

In the spaces provided below, write your own complete sentences using subordinate clauses of time, place, and action. Underline each subordinate clause. Try to use the clauses in all three positions: at the beginning, end, and middle of the sentence. Make your ten sentences hold together in a narrative or paragraph argument. Choose a subject that you know a good deal about, either through personal experience or through study. The better you know your subject the better your sentences will be. Identify your subordinate clauses, in the space provided, as to whether they are clauses of time, place,

_____ 1. _____

_____

_____ 2. _____

_____

_____ 3. _____

_____

_____ 4. _____

_____

_____ 5. _____

_____

_____ 6. _____

_____

_____ 7. _____

_____

_____   8. _____

             _____

_____   9. _____

             _____

_____   10. _____

             _____

12 Subordinate Clauses: Nouns and Adjectives

Subordinate clauses give many kinds of information. The subordinate clauses already mentioned, those that act as adverbs, give information about the action of the verb. They tell us about time, place, and action. Some subordinate clauses give us information about subjects, objects, or complements, and they are called adjective clauses. However, other clauses, the noun clauses, do not just give us additional information about subjects, objects, or complements—they can actually *be* the subjects, objects, or complements. First, we will examine the noun clause.

Subordinate clause: noun

The noun clause behaves just like the nouns you have already studied. It can be the subject of a predicate verb:

> That Rita won the election was certain.

In this sentence the predicate verb is "was." What was? The entire expression: "That Rita won the election." Note that the noun clause does not make a complete statement. It needs to be the subject of a verb (in this case) in order to make full sense.

The noun clause can be a noun complement if the same sentence is turned around:

> It was certain that Rita had won the election.

The subject of this sentence is "It." The predicate verb is "was." When you pose the question, "It was what?" the only answer must be the entire noun clause: "that Rita won the election."

In both of these examples, the predicate verb is a linking verb. You may wish to review Section I, Units 3 and 5 in order to keep the difference between action and linking verbs clear.

The third use for the noun clause is as an object. An action verb is needed for a noun clause to be an object. Using the same noun clause as in the examples above, we can choose from such action verbs as "imagine," "hope," "expect," and produce sentences:

Mr. Alvario hoped that Rita had won the election.

Jasper imagined that Rita had won the election.

Everyone expected that Rita had won the election.

"That" clauses are very often noun clauses. Here are some samples of typical "that" clauses:

that	+	subject	+	predicate
that		everyone		knew about the victory
that		we		could not tell them
that		people		enjoy gossip
that		our school		is becoming well known
that		basketball		makes some folks excited

Another common form for the noun clause is the "whoever" clause. The pattern for the "whoever" clause is the same as for the "that" clause:

whoever	+	subject	+	predicate
whoever		we		wanted
whoever		Inez		invited
whoever		they		sent for
whoever		Phyllis		had in mind

The "whoever" clause has one pattern that differs from the "that" clause. It is the pattern in which "whoever" is the subject. It works in this fashion:

subject	+	predicate
whoever		turned around
whoever		is arriving late
whoever		sees the train

Noun clauses of any kind usually come before or after the independent clause, but do not interrupt it, as many adverb clauses will. The examples that follow are noun clauses. They are underlined and their function is identified: subject (subj.), object (obj.), or complement (comp.). They are identified not to suggest that identification is so important by itself, but to establish the fact that these are indeed noun clauses. They become noun clauses because of their function as subject, object, or complement.

subj.   obj.
──────/────── 1. <u>Whoever saw Jasper last night</u> hoped <u>that he would not see him.</u>

obj.
────── 2. Jasper did not know <u>that it was Inez's uncle.</u>

subj.
────── 3. <u>Whatever Inez's uncle said</u> made Jasper uncomfortable.

comp.
────── 4. The fact was <u>that her uncle seemed to threaten him.</u>

obj.
────── 5. Eventually Jasper found out <u>whom he had seen.</u>

obj.
────── 6. That was <u>something</u> he wanted to forget.

obj.
────── 7. He knew <u>whatever Inez's uncle was doing was no good.</u>

obj.
────── 8. Actually, Inez's uncle Lou thought <u>that his surprise was now out in the open.</u>

obj.
────── 9. Jasper was embarrassed about <u>what he had thought.</u>

comp.
────── 10. All Lou had said was <u>that Jasper should keep his mouth shut.</u>

The spaces provided below will give you a chance to work with the noun clause. The first six spaces ask for noun clauses of a specific function: subject, object, complement. The next four spaces permit you to use noun clauses of your own choice of function. Try to make your sentences relate closely to one another as if they were forming a paragraph or telling a story.

subj.   1. _____

_____

comp.   2. _____

_____

obj.   3. _____

_____

obj.   4. _____

_____

subj.   5. _____

_____

6. _____

_____

7. _____

_____

8. _____

_____

9. _____

_____

10. _____

_____

Subordinate clause: adjective

While the noun clause *is* the subject, object, or complement, the adjective clause modifies the subject, object, or complement. It modifies a noun, thus giving information about who or what. The words that usually introduce an adjective clause are:

> who
> which
> that
> whose
> whom

Unlike noun clauses, adjective clauses usually come in the middle of a sentence because they are introduced by pronouns. A pronoun stands for, or refers to, a word or unspoken idea that is itself a noun. In the best-written sentences, the pronoun is clearly related to the noun it stands for. Often, it is right next to it, as in constructions such as:

> the man who
> the building, which

the idea that
the teacher whose
the friend whom

All of these are familiar patterns for the adjective clause because the word introducing the clause is about to give information about a man, a building, an idea, a teacher, and a friend—all of which are nouns.

The following are all adjective clauses, underlined, with the word they modify coming right before them. They are all very natural and ordinary constructions.

the woman who first climbed Chimborazo

people who need people

buildings whose architecture is marvelous

a person whom we all love

something that we all share

Notice that all the first words, the nouns modified by the adjective clauses, are either common nouns or abstract nouns. When using proper nouns, commas are used to set off the adjective clause. The pattern for modifying proper nouns is:

Jasper Paloma, whom everyone admired,

Saturday Night Live, which Rita and Inez watched,

Robert Frost, who once read poems at our school,

The Ramones, that Punk-rock group we heard last year,

Again, notice in the following examples that the adjective clauses are underlined and that they generally fall in the middle of the sentence.

1. We went to hear a rock group that everyone raved about.
2. Johnny Bizarre, whose name is a fake, was the leader.
3. Heavy Metal, which is not exactly my style, sounded sweet compared to this kind of music.
4. They had an electrical system whose output could have drowned out Niagara Falls.
5. All night long they played songs that meant nothing to me.
6. Then they played "Gotcha Baby," which has always been my tune.
7. Bizarre hit the chorus with a style of picking that I'd never seen before: he used a false tooth as a guitar pick.
8. He took everything in double time, which must have been tough.

9. It was a pace <u>that would have broken my wrist</u>, and I marveled at the drummer, <u>who had no trouble keeping the beat</u>.

10. I realized that any tune <u>that could survive the tooth-picking of Johnny Bizarre must be pure gold.</u>

▶ **POINTER**

Restrictive and Nonrestrictive Clauses

Most of the sentences above follow the patterns we have established. Number 10 has a noun clause as the object of the predicate verb, "realized." The adjective clause is inside it, modifying "tune." Number 8 is curious because the adjective clause modifies the entire preceding clause: the idea of playing fast, and not just the word "time." In such a case, use a comma to distinguish what is modified.

More importantly, two kinds of adjective clauses are used here: restrictive and nonrestrictive. These can give writers a bit of trouble because they are punctuated differently. *The restrictive clause provides information that is essential to the meaning of the sentence*—as in numbers 1, 4, 5, 7, the first adjective clause in 9, and 10. In these instances, no comma is needed because the information is crucial to the sentence.

The nonrestrictive clause provides interesting, but not essential, information. Therefore it is set off with commas, as in 2, 3, 6, and the second adjective clause in 9. You will also note that all adjective clauses coming after a proper name are nonrestrictive because the name itself restricts the meaning. The name is essential information; anything further is interesting but not essential.

Remember: if the information the clause gives is crucial to understanding the sentence, leave out the commas. If the information the clause gives can be left out without changing the meaning of the sentence, then use commas around it.

In the following spaces, write ten sentences that hold together as a narrative or a paragraph. Use as many adjective clauses as possible. Try to aim for variety, and try to include restrictive as well as nonrestrictive clauses.

1. _____

_____

2. _____

_____

3. _____

_____

4. _____

_____

5. _____

_____

6. _____

_____

7. _____

_____

8. _____

_____

9. _____

_____

10. _____

_____

In the following spaces, write five connected sentences about a single topic. Try to use *both* noun clauses and adjective clauses. Aim for variety and for ease of expression. Underline the noun clauses and box the adjective clauses.

1. _____

_____

_____

2. _____

_____

_____

3. _____

_____

_____

4. _____

_____

_____

5. _____

_____

_____

13 The Prepositional Phrase

The prepositional phrase begins with the word that gives it its name: the preposition. Most of us use prepositional phrases as much in speech as we do in writing. Most of your own writing depends on prepositional phrases to supply crucial information about both the subject and the predicate verb in a form that is easy to comprehend.

All the following phrases are prepositional. They have no subject and no predicate verb. The form of all prepositional phrases is:

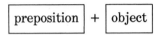

All objects are nouns or pronouns. They can be the names of abstract ideas; they can be common names; they can be proper names. You may want to review Section I, Units 1 and 5 before continuing. Note that the most common prepositions are: at, to, for, of, with, in, and by. Examine the following examples closely. The prepositions are underlined.

1. with Jasper, Rita, and Inez
2. to the corner store
3. by the music display
4. in time
5. with certain music
6. at the same place
7. of no consequence
8. from Rita's own family
9. on the money
10. for a gift

In the spaces provided below, write ten prepositional phrases of your own. Try to relate them to each other if you can. Also, try to use at least one different preposition than the examples used above. Read through this book or another book looking for new prepositions to use.

1. _____

2. _____

3. _____

4. _____

5. _____

6. _____

7. _____

8. _____

9. _____

10. _____

Have your work checked carefully. If it is satisfactory, continue. If not, review the introductory material and study the Prepositional Phrase Pointer that follows.

▶ **PREPOSITIONAL PHRASE POINTER**

The first part of a prepositional phrase raises a question. The second part answers it. When we begin a phrase with a preposition such as "to," we are setting up expectations. We naturally ask, "to what?" or, "to whom?" The answer in number 2 on page 73 is "the corner store." The preposition asks a question and its object answers it.

The prepositional phrase has one interesting and very useful quality: it can be strung together with other prepositional phrases to provide even more information than one phrase can. The pattern for this, which needs no special punctuation, is:

| prepositional phrase | + | prepositional phrase | + | prepositional phrase |

An example would be:

    with Jasper and Rita by the music display in the record store.

These three phrases give information about who, where, and when. More examples of stringing prepositional phrases together follow.

1. by the path in the village
2. in time for a really good meal at home
3. with the present for Phil on his birthday in March of this year
4. by the stream in the mountains
5. at the corner by Rita's

In the spaces that follow, try stringing prepositional phrases together. In the last space, see how many prepositional phrases you can link together without losing meaning and without being repetitious.

1. _____

2. _____

3. _____

4. _____

5. _____

_____

_____

Prepositional phrases of time, place, manner, condition

The fact that they give information about time, place, manner, and condition makes prepositional phrases very useful. The lists following are only some of the most useful prepositions of time, place, manner, and condition, but they are very important.

Prepositions of	*time*	*place*	*manner*	*condition*
	after	near	with	if
	before	by	without	unless
	since	through	in	except
	until	toward	by	but
	up to	at	because of	on condition of

The following examples of prepositional phrases give information concerning time, place, manner, and condition. Here we are not too concerned with identifying each of these functions, but we are concerned with mastering the use of such prepositions as those we have listed. Examine these samples. The prepositions are underlined.

1. after dinner
2. toward the highway
3. because of the delay
4. without a song
5. up to this morning

6. since breakfast
7. unless well protected
8. at Herbie's place
9. until nightfall
10. except the stove

In the spaces provided, write your own prepositional phrases of time, place, manner, and condition.

1. _____

2. _____

3. _____

4. _____

5. _____

6. _____

7. _____

8. _____

9. _____

10. _____

Using prepositional phrases in a sentence

It is very important to be able to write prepositional phrases, but it is even more important to be able to use them in sentences. When they modify subjects and objects, prepositional phrases are called adjective phrases. When they modify predicate verbs, prepositional phrases are called adverb phrases. Most of the prepositional phrases of time, place, manner, and condition are adverb phrases, and they therefore will modify predicate verbs. In the following examples, the prepositional phrases are underlined. In the spaces before each sentence identify the prepositional phrases as adjective phrases or adverb phrases.

_____ / _____ 1. The man in the bank walked off with the money.

_____ 2. No one near the scene saw what happened.

_____ 3. The police officer on the beat was surprised.

_____ 4. He started out after the thief.

_____ 5. By the time he rounded the corner, the officer had help.

_____ 6. A brigade of middle-schoolers had seen the man running.

_____ 7. Somehow the thief lost his balance and fell in their midst.

_____ 8. The bag of money went flying.

_____ / _____ / _____ 9. Across the street, in the street, and on the sidewalk, the middle-schoolers chased the money.

_____ / _____ 10. Meantime, the thief could not get untangled from the tiny students, and he got caught by Mrs. Robinson's seventh graders.

As you can see from this sample, very important information finds its way into prepositional phrases. You have space below for a paragraph of five sentences. Use as many prepositional phrases of time, place, manner, and condition as possible. Be prepared to identify your phrases as adjective phrases or as adverb phrases.

1. _____

_____

2. _____

_____

3. _____

_____

4. _____

_____

5. _____

_____

14 The Participial Phrase

A participial phrase usually begins with a participle. The participle is the form of the verb used to make perfect and imperfect tenses. We worked with these forms in Section I, Unit 3, "The Simple Predicate." A review of that unit will help you with what follows. We will begin with the present participle, the form ending with "-ing." The structure of the participial phrase is:

$$\boxed{\text{participle}} + \boxed{\text{object}}$$

Some examples of the participial phrase are:

<u>having</u> a bad cold

<u>wanting</u> more soup

<u>sensing</u> the danger

<u>unveiling</u> the monument

<u>expecting</u> a different person

<u>seeing</u> me

The participle is underlined in each example. As in the prepositional phrase, the participle sets up expectations. If we begin a phrase with "having," we naturally want to know what completes it: "Having what?" The object tells us the what. You will see, too, that each of these participles needs a subject. We want to know who is "sensing the danger," or who is "expecting a different person," or who is "seeing me." In order to write clearly, we must place the subject of the participial phrase immediately before the phrase or immediately after it. Any other placement creates confusion and uncertainty. Two structures are possible; study each carefully, particularly for the manner in which the commas are used.

$$\boxed{\text{subject}} + \boxed{,} + \boxed{\text{participial phrase}} + \boxed{,} + \boxed{\text{predicate.}}$$

$$\boxed{\text{participial phrase}} + \boxed{,} + \boxed{\text{subject}} + \boxed{\text{predicate.}}$$

Both forms are acceptable and both are used frequently by all writers.

▶ **POINTER**

Dangling Participial Phrase

You may have heard of the *dangling participial phrase*. It is a term used when the participial phrase does not have its subject immediately before or after it. If you follow the forms given immediately above, you will have no trouble with dangling participial phrases. *Remember: keep the subject of the participle as close to it as possible*, and you will not cause confusion.

Study the underlined examples of the participial phrases that follow. Each modifies its subject, which is either just before or just after the phrase and is boxed. Since participial phrases modify a subject, they are considered adjective phrases. Because they are considered adjective phrases, it is very important to keep them close to the word they modify.

1. <u>Seeing Randy up close,</u> ⟨Jenny⟩ began to think twice.

2. ⟨Randy,⟩ <u>noting her look,</u> wondered what was wrong.

3. <u>Hoping he wasn't hurt,</u> ⟨Jenny⟩ turned to go.

4. <u>Shaving this morning,</u> ⟨Randy⟩ took off only half his beard.

5. $\boxed{\text{Jenny,}}$ <u>laughing behind her hand</u>, tried to get away.

6. But $\boxed{\text{Randy,}}$ <u>holding her with one hand</u>, wouldn't let her go.

7. <u>Finally explaining it all</u>, $\boxed{\text{Jenny}}$ was able to laugh out loud.

8. $\boxed{\text{Randy,}}$ <u>now understanding the problem</u>, could laugh, too.

You should be prepared to note two things about the examples. First, in number 3, "Hoping he wasn't hurt" uses a noun clause as the object of the participle. As in prepositional phrases, this is a common pattern. In numbers 7 and 8 the phrases do not begin with participles. They begin with the adverb subordinators "finally" and "now." Again, this is a common pattern. The phrases are still participial.

In the spaces below, write five sentences using participial phrases. Be sure three of your phrases follow their subject and two come before it. Underline the participle and box the subject.

1. _____

_____

2. _____

_____

3. _____

_____

4. _____

_____

5. _____

_____

Participial phrases and prepositional phrases

One interesting structure that we use often is this:

$$\boxed{\text{participle}} + \boxed{\text{prepositional phrase}}$$

Since a prepositional phrase can be used as a noun phrase, it can be an object. Thus, in the structure above, it functions as the object of a participle. Some examples follow:

> Understanding in depth, I
> Sinking by degrees, I
> Staying at home, I
> Crying after all, I
> Hiding under the couch, I

This pattern is generally used more with the past tense participle than with the present tense participle. Therefore, before you try to write this pattern yourself, examine the forms the participle takes in different tenses.

Present tense	*Past tense*	*Present perfect tense*
1. seeing	seen	having seen
2. deciding	decided	having decided
3. hearing	heard	having heard
4. being	been	having been
5. doing	done	having done
6. leaving	left	having left
7. needing	needed	having needed
8. forgetting	forgotten	having forgotten
9. losing	lost	having lost
10. knowing	known	having known

We can make participial phrases using all these tenses. The past tense form and the present perfect tense form both take the pattern of

$$\boxed{\text{participle}} + \boxed{\text{prepositional phrase}}$$

in a very natural way. In numbers 1, 5, 6, 9, and 10 below, this is the pattern that is followed. In each case the participle is underlined. Study each example to see what the subject of the participle is, what tense the participle is, and what the object of the participle is. Be prepared to identify each, should you be asked.

1. The *Marietta*, <u>tossed</u> by the storm, limped to shelter.

2. <u>Thinking</u> it was lost, the *Marietta*'s owners sold out their shares.

3. The new owner, Captain Bill, <u>expecting</u> nothing, went looking for it.

4. <u>Needing</u> repairs, the *Marietta* could not move for three months.

5. <u>Having searched</u> for three months himself, Captain Bill gave up.

6. The news of the *Marietta*'s survival, <u>having finally arrived</u> by a friendly vessel, cheered Captain Bill immensely.

7. <u>Realizing</u> he was going to do very well for himself, Captain Bill thought of selling the ship for a profit.

8. The *Marietta*, now <u>known</u> to be on its way home, became a valuable piece of property.

9. Its original owners, <u>motivated</u> by their affection for the ship, offered Bill a good price, which he refused.

10. Captain Bill, ultimately <u>lured</u> by the thought of his own command, decided to keep the ship for himself and enter the coal trade.

▶ **PARTICIPLE POINTER**

The examples above contain participles with prepositional phrases as their objects, with single nouns as their objects, and with noun clauses as their objects. You should practice with all three. You will note, too, that stylistically, it is difficult to write a succession of sentences with participial phrases without becoming repetitive. The lesson to learn from this is that variety is necessary in all writing. For the sake of these exercises, however, repeating the pattern can be useful. Note, too, that there are predicate verbs in these sentences whose form is the same as the participle. In number 9, "offered" and "refused" have the same form as "motivated." But "motivated" is a participle because it is an adjective and it modifies "owners." "Offered" is a verb because it expresses the action of a subject, "owners." The subject of "refused" is "he." The distinction between the genuine participle and the past tense verb is very subtle. When in doubt, ask yourself if a real action is expressed by the word that could be either a participle or a predicate verb. The participle describes something; the predicate verb expresses a real action.

In the following spaces, write five sentences connected in meaning. Use as many participial phrases and as many tenses of the participles as possible. Be sure to keep the subject of the participle as close to it as possible. Underline each participle. Refer back to all the examples in this unit before you begin writing.

1. _____

   _____

2. _____

   _____

3. _____

   _____

4. _____

   _____

5. _____

   _____

15 The Infinitive Phrase

The infinitive is the basic form of the verb. It cannot, however, be a predicate verb because it does not express a completed action; rather, it names the action. Instead of being a predicate verb, the infinitive can be a noun, an adjective, or an adverb. In a sense, these are the most difficult facts we must learn about the infinitive. The simpler fact is that of recognition. We can recognize the infinitive easily because it is always in this structure:

$$\boxed{\text{to}} + \boxed{\text{verb}}$$

to   go
to   see

The following list of infinitives should help clarify their nature. You have probably seen them all and used them all before.

1.	to be	8.	to neglect
2.	to need	9.	to help
3.	to find	10.	to respect
4.	to sense	11.	to applaud
5.	to have	12.	to apprehend
6.	to argue	13.	to resist
7.	to respond	14.	to accept

Before going further, write your own infinitives in the spaces provided. Use different infinitives from those above.

1. _____   4. _____

2. _____   5. _____

3. _____   6. _____

The infinitive phrase, like the prepositional phrase and the participial phrase, adds an object to the infinitive. The structure is:

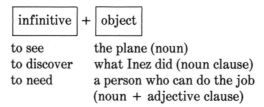

| infinitive | + | object |

to see   the plane (noun)
to discover   what Inez did (noun clause)
to need   a person who can do the job
                (noun + adjective clause)

Describing the grammar of some infinitive phrases may sometimes be tricky. But in the ordinary circumstances of writing, using such phrases is not as difficult as we might expect, even when they contain noun or adjective clauses. Consider the following infinitive phrases carefully.

1. to infiltrate behind "enemy" lines
2. to try some espionage tactics
3. to need training
4. to hope that we are not discovered
5. to avoid the searchlight
6. to lie low
7. to recognize the commanding officer's gruff voice
8. to wish we were still safe at home in college
9. to surrender to the "enemy"
10. to be glad it's only "war games" and not the real thing

In the spaces provided, write your own infinitive phrases. If possible, try to relate them all in meaning, as in the examples above. Use as much variety as possible. Remember that you are writing infinitive phrases, not clauses or sentences.

1. _____

2. _____

3. _____

4. _____

5. _____

6. _____

7. _____

8. _____

9. _____

10. _____

▶ **PUNCTUATION POINTER**

You may have already realized that the infinitive phrase is very flexible. You can begin with an infinitive, add a prepositional phrase as its modifier, or add a noun or adjective clause as its object without any special punctuation. Just as with the predicate verb and its object, no comma separates the infinitive and its object.

Using the infinitive phrase in a sentence

No special punctuation is needed to use an infinitive phrase in a sentence. An infinitive phrase can be the subject of a predicate verb, the object of a predicate verb, or the complement of a predicate verb. It can also modify a predicate verb and, thus, be an adverb. The infinitive phrase is underlined in the following sentences, and its function, subject, object, complement, or adverb, is identified.

subj.   1. <u>To want a good job</u> is normal.

obj.   2. Jaime Melodia wanted <u>to get a good job</u>.

comp.   3. Jaime's wish was <u>to work on the newspaper</u>.

adv.   4. He was anxious <u>to have a good interview</u>.

The infinitive phrase may also be used as the object of a preposition:

He wanted nothing except <u>to be a reporter</u>.

But such uses are relatively rare and usually don't cause us problems in writing. In the following sentences, the infinitive phrases are underlined. In the space before each sentence, establish the way in which each infinitive phrase is used by writing subj., obj., comp., or adv.

_____   1. Mr. Alvario wanted <u>to watch the TV news report</u>.

_____   2. He was eager <u>to see if he was on it</u>.

_____   3. The program was <u>to be shown at 6:15 P.M.</u>

_____/_____   4. <u>To see the news at that hour</u>, he had <u>to hurry home</u>.

_____   5. <u>To see the beginning</u> would be impossible.

_____   6. But <u>to miss it</u> would have been terrible.

_____   7. He appeared in front of the cameras <u>to speak out on higher education</u>.

_____   8. His fight was <u>to stop further budget cuts</u>.

_____/_____   9. <u>To cut the budget further</u> would have been <u>to cripple the language program entirely</u>.

_____/_____   10. Luckily, he managed <u>to get home in time</u> <u>to hear his interview</u>.

In the spaces below, use infinitive phrases in sentences that form a single paragraph. Aim at variety so that your sentences do not sound dull and artificial. This is a tall order, so you will have to work very carefully. Be sure to use the infinitive phrase in many different ways: as subject, object, complement, and adverb.

1. _____

_____

2. _____

_____

3. _____

_____

4. _____

_____

5. _____

_____

6. _____

_____

7. _____

_____

8. _____

_____

9. _____

_____

10. _____

_____

As a final check, underline the infinitive phrases in the following sentences. Be prepared to identify their function in the sentence.

1. The Canadians seem to have a language problem.

2. One part of Canada is content to speak only English.

3. Another part, Quebec, wants to speak French.

4. The result is that schoolchildren have to learn both languages.

5. To learn two languages is no hardship for the young.

6. But to begin another language is very difficult when one is over forty.

7. One solution is to have two nations, one French, one English.

8. To propose such a solution is to anger many Canadians.

9. After all, the United States went to war to preserve the Union.

10. Let us hope the Canadians can learn how to avoid a civil war over this issue.

16 The Gerund Phrase

A gerund is a word that has the form of the present participle, but is used as a noun. It is always the name of an action or state of being. "Going," "being," "running," "having," "moving" are all gerunds when they name their respective actions. A gerund can act as subject, object, and complement. It may be the object of a predicate verb or the object of a preposition. Consider the following phrases. Each is the name of an action and each follows the familiar pattern.

gerund	+	object
driving		a car (noun)
doing		a favor (noun)
understanding		everything he said (noun clause)
approving		what we already agreed upon (noun clause)

The gerund phrases that follow are all the names of actions. The objects of the gerunds themselves, whether single words or entire noun clauses, help make the action named much more specific.

1. riding a bicycle
2. taking over the store his father left him
3. having enough money to ask Inez out
4. possessing enough pride to turn him down
5. coping with reality
6. studying for finals
7. writing term papers
8. doing things right
9. solving real problems
10. having no doubts about the future

Write your own gerund phrases in the spaces indicated. Be sure to review each by asking whether it is really the name of an action. Make your objects clarify the exact nature of the action.

1. _____

2. _____

3. _____

4. _____

5. _____

6. _____

7. _____

8. _____

9. _____

10. _____

Using the gerund phrase in a sentence

Since the gerund phrase is a noun, it can be used as the subject, object, or complement of a predicate verb and as the object of a preposition. Each of the following sample sentences has its gerund phrase underlined. The function of the gerund phrase is indicated before each sentence.

obj. of prep.
_____   1. By riding the bicycle I saved some gas.

subj. of verb
_____   2. My riding the bicycle saved some gas.

obj. of verb
_____   3. The regulations prohibit our driving cars.

comp. of verb
_____   4. What the dean liked was our riding bicycles to school.

▶ **GERUND POINTER**

Gerunds have objects whose form is the same as other objects. But gerunds also have subjects whose form is very different from other subjects. In numbers 2, 3, and 4 above, the subjects of the gerunds are "My," "our," and "our." *They are possessive in form. All subjects of gerunds must be in the possessive case.* That means we must use pronouns such as: my, your, his, hers, its, our, and their, and the possessive form of proper names: "Leonard's," "Alfred's," "Romeo's," "Christina's," "Maud's"; and common names: "men's," "women's," "the bodyguards'," "the priest's." Note the subjects in the next group of sample sentences. Each is in the possessive case.

The examples below have gerund phrases underlined. You may be asked whether the phrase is functioning as a subject, an object, or a complement of a predicate verb or if it is an object of a preposition. Examine each to be sure you know.

_____   1. Saving petroleum is likely to be important in the 1980s.

_____   2. One method of conservation is driving less.

____/____/____ 3. Traveling less, moving less often, and staying at home will be more of the American way of life.

____/____ 4. In saving fuel we may help in saving the future.

_____ 5. Finding new sources of energy will be a national priority.

_____/_____/_____ 6. Tapping the sun's energy by improving solar panels or by inventing new conversion methods may help us keep fuel prices down.

_____/_____ 7. Our converting to solar energy may help our rationing of other fuels.

_____/_____ 8. Nations with large oil reserves probably will not curtail their driving or their burning of fossil fuels.

_____ 9. Rich nations without oil reserves will be forced into spending more and more of their wealth on oil.

_____/_____ 10. Poor nations without oil reserves will be prevented from developing their industries and from sharing fully in the world's wealth.

When you write your own sentences below, underline your gerund phrases. Make every effort to connect your sentences in a coherent paragraph, and be sure you can explain how the gerund phrases are used in the sentence. Be sure, too, that the subjects of your gerund phrases are in the possessive case.

1. _____

2. _____

3. _____

4. _____

5. _____

6. _____

7. _____

8. _____

9. _____

10. _____

Gerunds can be tricky because their form is the same as the present participle and the present imperfect tense. For that reason, you will find some of the following examples difficult. Your job is to underline the gerund phrases. You should also be able to identify the present imperfect tense predicate verbs and the participles.

1. Studying for exams is not getting any easier for me.

2. Starting out two years ago, I could get excited by studying.

3. Even staying up late has lost its charm for me.

4. I would rather be reading for fun than studying for a test.

5. But you don't get college credit by reading for fun.

6. So maybe I will try studying a bit harder only because it is becoming such a chore.

7. Who knows? Studying may get easier next year.

SECTION III

Principles
of
Coordination

17 Coordinating Subjects and Predicates

When structures of the same kind are linked in a sentence, the process is called coordination. We can coordinate any of the basic parts of a sentence: subjects, predicates, and their modifiers; phrases and subordinate clauses; even two or more independent clauses.

When two or more of the same sentence parts are linked, a special kind of linking word is used: the coordinating conjunction. The main coordinating conjunctions are:

and, or, nor, but, for, yet, so

Coordinating conjunctions can only be used when two sentence parts of the same value are linked. That is, the patterns should be:

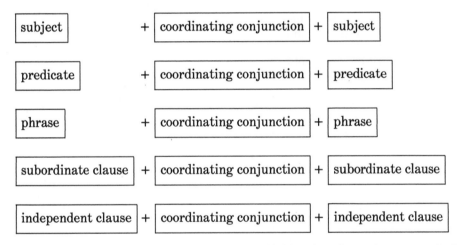

Not only should the sentence parts you are linking be of equal grammatical value; they should also be of equal importance to the meaning of your sentence.

Coordination is a very useful, and even necessary, device to bring clarity and conciseness to your writing. For instance, think how awkward it would be to write:

Joe sauntered down the street.
Elvira sauntered down the street.

Obviously, you can avoid repetition and improve your statement by coordinating the subjects:

Joe and Elvira sauntered down the street.

Coordinating subjects

When two subjects are joined, the sentence pattern is as follows:

| subject | + | coordinating conjunction | + | subject | + | predicate |

In the following sentences both subjects are boxed. The underlined word linking them is a coordinating conjunction.

| Cats | and | dogs | make nice pets.

The | men | and | women | attended class.

▶ **AGREEMENT POINTER**

When two singular subjects are joined by "and," the predicate verb that follows must be plural:

> David and Joel exercise daily.
> The classroom and the hall are joined by a door.

Keep this in mind when you write your own sentences with coordinated subjects.

Sometimes two subjects are linked by special paired conjunctions such as:

> either . . . or
> neither . . . nor

In these cases, the predicate verb that follows is singular if the subjects are singular:

> Either Liz or Ann is going to Boston next week.
> Neither Larry nor Mark sews very well.

In the first sentence only *one* person is going to Boston; in the second sentence, *neither* man sews well; in both sentences, then, the predicate verb is singular.

If both subjects are plural, however, the predicate remains plural:

> Neither the Smiths nor the Washingtons are joining us tonight.

In the sentences below, write a suitable predicate verb in the space provided; be sure your choice makes sense, is in the present tense, and is in proper agreement with its subject or subjects. The first two sentences are filled in to show you how to proceed.

1. The men and women of America ___have___ the right to vote.

2. Neither the table nor the chair ___is___ made of wood.

3. The house and the barn _____ a new coat of paint.

4. Either the apple or the pear _____ good.

5. Neither the spoons nor the knives _____ clean.

6. The car and the bus _____ at the corner.

7. Either pencils or pens _____ on paper.

8. The red jacket and the blue pants _____ in the washing machine.

9. Neither Dolly Parton nor Johnny Cash _____ in live performances.

10. The Empire State Building and the World Trade Towers _____ in New York.

Coordinating predicates

When two predicate verbs are joined, the sentence pattern is as follows:

| subject | + | predicate | + | coordinating conjunction | + | predicate |

In the following sentences both predicates are boxed, and the coordinating conjunction is underlined.

The President | lifts | his pen and | signs | the treaty.

That performer | sings | well but | dances | better.

I $\boxed{\text{found}}$ the key <u>and</u> $\boxed{\text{started}}$ the car.

Remember that both predicates must be in agreement with the subject of the sentence. As before, special paired conjunctions may be used:

I <u>neither</u> $\boxed{\text{liked}}$ him <u>nor</u> $\boxed{\text{wanted}}$ him around.

José <u>either</u> $\boxed{\text{sleeps}}$ <u>or</u> $\boxed{\text{eats}}$ at this hour of the afternoon.

In the sentences below, add predicates in the spaces provided. Be sure both predicates agree with the subject of the sentence.

1. The cars in the street _____ and _____ .

2. Many of my fellow students _____ and _____ in class.

3. Jasper, my mother's cousin, either _____ or _____ when he is at our house.

4. The man in the theater balcony neither _____ nor

_____ the act on the stage.

5. Al Martinez _____ well but _____ better.

18 Coordinating Independent Clauses

The pattern for joining two independent clauses into a sentence is:

| independent clause | + | coordinating conjunction | + | independent clause |

In the following sentences the independent clauses are boxed. The word linking them is a coordinating conjunction and is underlined.

1. | The union wanted to strike, | but | the workers could not agree. |

2. | Some wanted a raise in pay, | and | others wanted better medical coverage. |

3. | They would have to come to some agreement, | or | they wouldn't get anything. |

4. | The union organizer was helpful, | for | he had been through negotiations before. |

5. | He wouldn't let them fight, | nor | would he allow them to give up. |

▶ **PUNCTUATION POINTER**

A comma follows the first independent clause and comes before the coordinating conjunction. Sometimes the sentence is just as clear if the comma is left out, but only if the independent clauses are very short. The conjunction "nor" always has a comma in front of it, but you will note that the pattern after "nor" is | predicate | + | subject | (as in number 5 above). This is the opposite of the normal pattern after most conjunctions.

In the spaces provided below, use each of the seven coordinating conjunctions listed at the beginning of Unit 17 to join two independent clauses. Box each independent clause and underline the coordinating conjunction. Try to relate the sentences to each other as if they were part of a story.

1. _____

2. _____

3. _____

4. _____

5. _____

6. _____

7. _____

After you have written the sentences, go over each clause to be sure of two things: (1) that each clause has both a subject and a predicate; (2) that each clause is independent and not subordinate.

Like subjects and predicates, independent clauses can also be joined by paired conjunctions. The only problem these conjunctions are likely to cause is that the ‾subject‾ + ‾predicate‾ pattern is sometimes reversed, as it is when "nor" is used. Otherwise, the pattern for using these paired conjunctions is:

<u>either</u> independent clause <u>or</u> independent clause

Some examples of this pattern follow. The independent clauses are boxed, and the conjunctions are underlined.

<u>Either</u> I go home right away, <u>or</u> I stick around here until dinnertime.

<u>Neither</u> will I praise the Democrats, <u>nor</u> will I condemn the

Republicans.

Not only | do I have enough money to go to New York, | but | I can | also

go to Paris.

▶ **PUNCTUATION POINTER**

Paired coordinating conjunctions are separated by commas. There is always a comma right before the second conjunction.

Use each of the three paired conjunctions in sentences of your own below. Try to write interesting sentences.

1. _____

2. _____

3. _____

▶ **PUNCTUATION POINTER**

The Comma Splice

Many writers are haunted by the comma splice, which is nothing more than leaving out the coordinating conjunction. *Two independent clauses cannot be joined by just a comma.* This is one of the most important rules to remember in your own writing.

For a fuller discussion of this problem, see Section I, Unit 8.

19 Coordinating Phrases

Participial phrases, prepositional phrases, infinitive phrases, and gerund phrases are linked to phrases of their own kind by the same coordinating conjunctions mentioned in the previous units. Keep in mind that the phrases must be of the same kind; that is, a participial phrase must be coordinated with another participial phrase, a prepositional phrase with a prepositional phrase, and so on. Before you go on with this unit, it might help you to review Units 13, 14, 15, 16, where these phrases are discussed in detail.

The basic pattern for coordinating phrases is:

$$\boxed{\text{phrase}} + \boxed{\text{coordinating conjunction}} + \boxed{\text{phrase}}$$

Notice that the structure you get from using this pattern is not a complete sentence, it is only part of a sentence. A phrase lacks either a subject or a predicate, so it cannot be a sentence even if it is linked to another phrase. In order to make this pattern into a sentence, we must join it to an independent clause.

Coordinating participial phrases

In the examples below, the participial phrases are boxed for easy identification, while the coordinating conjunctions are underlined. Note that both phrases must have the same subject; otherwise, the sentence wouldn't make sense.

1. $\boxed{\text{Going home}}$ <u>and</u> $\boxed{\text{brushing my teeth,}}$ I got ready for the dance.

2. $\boxed{\text{Cleaned up}}$ <u>and</u> $\boxed{\text{dressed to kill,}}$ my date met me at the door.

3. $\boxed{\text{Both dancing every dance}}$ <u>and</u> $\boxed{\text{singing along with the band,}}$ we had a good time.

4. $\boxed{\text{Elated by our applause}}$ <u>but</u> $\boxed{\text{exhausted by their efforts,}}$ the band members played on.

5. <u>Neither</u> $\boxed{\text{wanting to go}}$ <u>nor</u> $\boxed{\text{being able to stay,}}$ everyone felt dejected at closing time.

In each space below write two participial phrases, link them with a coordinating conjunction, and follow them with an independent clause. Be sure your phrases are genuine participial phrases and that both of them refer to the same subject. Use a variety of coordinating conjunctions. Put a box around each participial phrase; underline the conjunctions. Try to develop your sentences into a coherent paragraph.

1. _____

2. _____

3. _____

4. _____

5. _____

Coordinating prepositional phrases

The basic principle for coordinating prepositional phrases is the same as that for coordinating participial phrases, and the same coordinating conjunctions are used. One point to keep in mind is that these conjunctions often link prepositional phrases that start with the same preposition. Pairs such as these are common:

> with me or with you
> in peace or in war

But coordinating conjunctions can link prepositional phrases that start with different prepositions, too. These examples are also common:

> from your friend Alma and with my love
> at home but not in bed

Study the examples below. The prepositional phrases are boxed and the coordinating conjunctions are underlined.

1. He will give the prize either | to me | <u>or</u> | to you. |

2. The prize is | for the best essay | <u>and</u> | for the best speech. |

3. It is given <u>not only</u> | by the school | <u>but also</u> | by the community. |

4. I gave my speech | from memory | <u>and</u> | with ease. |

5. It was received <u>neither</u> | with enthusiasm | <u>nor</u> | with applause. |

▶ **PUNCTUATION POINTER**

No special punctuation is needed when linking prepositional phrases to one another. Do not use commas here.

In the spaces below, write sentences in which you use two coordinated prepositional phrases. Use a variety of prepositions and a variety of coordinating conjunctions. Box each prepositional phrase and underline each coordinating conjunction. As usual, try to develop your sentences into a coherent paragraph.

1. _____

2. _____

3. _____

4. _____

5. _____

Coordinating infinitive phrases

Infinitive phrases are also coordinated with conjunctions. The same principles for joining prepositional phrases apply to joining infinitive phrases. The
following examples of infinitive phrases coordinated with one another have
the phrases boxed and the coordinating conjunctions underlined. Notice that
both coordinated phrases serve the same grammatical function; that is, both
serve as an object complement of the same verb, or both serve as an adverb
modifier of the same verb. This sameness of function is an important basic
principle of coordination.

1. My Uncle Toby learned to appreciate good music and to play

good piano when he was young.

2. His father told him either to listen or practice for an hour each day.

3. He played not only to get better but also to enjoy himself.

4. To join a band and to go on tour were his major goals.

5. He wanted neither to participate in sports nor to read many books.

   As a review, ask yourself how the coordinated sets of infinitive phrases
are used in each of the above examples. Are they the subjects of the
sentence? Objects of the verb? Adverb modifiers? Again, notice that both
phrases are used in the same way in each sentence.
   In the spaces provided link your own infinitive phrases. Try to use them
in a variety of ways: as subjects, objects, adverb modifiers, and so on. Box
the infinitive phrases and underline the coordinating conjunctions. Relate
your sentences so that they tell a story.

1. _____

_____

2. _____

_____

3. _____

_____

4. _____

_____

5. _____

_____

Coordinating gerund phrases

The principle of coordinating gerund phrases is the same as that for infinitive phrases. As before, both the coordinated phrases will serve the same grammatical function in the sentence. Since gerund phrases are verbal nouns, this means that both will be the subject of the same verb, the object of the same verb, the object of a preposition, and so on.

In the following examples, the gerund phrases are boxed and the coordinating conjunctions are underlined. Ask yourself how each set of phrases functions grammatically in the sentence. Notice that both phrases in the coordinated set serve the same function.

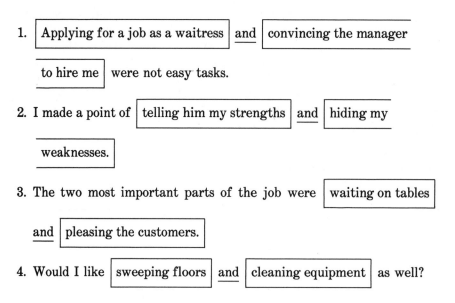

1. Applying for a job as a waitress and convincing the manager to hire me were not easy tasks.

2. I made a point of telling him my strengths and hiding my weaknesses.

3. The two most important parts of the job were waiting on tables and pleasing the customers.

4. Would I like sweeping floors and cleaning equipment as well?

5. After ┃ thinking it over ┃ and after ┃ talking with other waitresses, ┃

I decided not to take the job.

In the spaces provided below write your own coordinated gerund phrases. Check to make sure that they are gerund phrases and not participial phrases. Box the gerund phrases and underline the coordinating conjunctions. As in preceding exercises, relate the sentences so that they tell a story.

1. _____

_____

2. _____

_____

3. _____

_____

4. _____

_____

5. _____

_____

20 Coordinating Subordinate Clauses

Coordinating conjunctions can be used to link two or more subordinate clauses. The conjunctions we have mentioned—and, or, nor, but, yet, for, so —and most of the paired conjunctions work the same way for subordinate clauses as they do for independent clauses. The patterns for complete sentences using two subordinate clauses linked together would be:

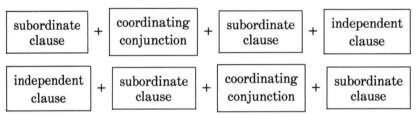

As the patterns indicate, the linked subordinate clauses can come before or after the independent clause. The sentences below illustrate both patterns. The independent clauses are underlined, the subordinate clauses are boxed, the conjunctions stand alone. Study the examples carefully.

1. Since Luther has gone and since Luella is about to finish, you can have your turn now.

2. You will find that starting isn't easy and that finishing is even harder.

3. You will run either until you finish or until you drop.

4. You should move around not only before you run the race but after you cross the finish line.

5. When you have had your turn, and when everyone else has had his or hers, the race will be over.

Write your own sentences below with linked subordinate clauses and an independent clause. Underline the independent clauses, box both the subordinate clauses, and leave the conjunctions unmarked. Vary your sentence structure, placing linked subordinate clauses at the beginning of some sentences, and at the end of other sentences. Try to develop a continuous story with your sentences.

1. _____

_____

2. _____

_____

3. _____

_____

4. _____

_____

5. _____

_____

SECTION IV

Proofreading the Sentence

21 Proofreading the Sentence

It is safe to say that very few people write flawless sentences the first time they try to write down their thoughts. Getting the idea written down is of primary importance; matters of punctuation, agreement, and sentence structure are usually of secondary interest.

Once the basic ideas are expressed, however, you must turn your attention to editing the sentences. This involves checking punctuation, making sure that sentences are complete and do not run on, correcting problems of verb and pronoun agreement, and so on. Learning to write grammatically perfect sentences is not an empty exercise. It is an attempt to express the writer's thoughts in their clearest form, and to eliminate basic errors that annoy the reader and obscure the meaning of the material.

One of your most important tasks as a beginning writer is to recognize the kind of errors you usually make and to develop strategies for correcting them. The exercises in this section are designed to help you do this.

Before you proceed, you might want to review some text and some pointers in the previous units. For your convenience, these units are listed below:

Proofreading for punctuation

Punctuation can cause beginning writers a lot of problems. Sometimes the reaction is "Why bother to punctuate?" But a properly punctuated sentence fulfills the expectations of your reader. It clarifies the meaning of your sentence so that the reader does not have to reread it to understand what is happening.

Capital letters

While capital letters are not often a problem, you should be aware that their absence can confuse your reader. If you leave out the capital letter at the beginning of a sentence, your reader may at first assume that it is a continuation of the previous sentence. He or she may have to reread the sentence to understand what is going on. If you fail to capitalize a proper noun, the reader may at first think that it is a common noun. Again, rereading may be required.

In the following exercise, capital letters have been left out. Decide where they are needed, and rewrite the paragraph with proper capitals in the space provided below. Notice how much clearer your rewritten paragraph is.

when sandy and i were younger, we were always in trouble. one saturday afternoon, sandy dropped her shoes over the balcony of the woodstock imperial theatre, where we had gone to see saturday night fever, a movie starring john travolta. she sent me down to retrieve the shoes, causing me great embarrassment. another time, i spilled a whole bottle of her mother's charlie perfume all over her rug. mrs. landry was very angry, and wouldn't speak to me for days. our biggest escapade was when we decided to pretend we were tom sawyer and huckleberry finn. we packed some food and some clothes and camped down by five mile river, a few miles from our home. our parents didn't know where we were. mr. landry called chief hector bombasi of the newtown police, who happened to be a friend of his. when they found us, sandy and i were too tired and cold to worry about their scolding. we were both grounded for the whole month of may. after that, we decided that getting into trouble was more trouble than it was worth.

_____

_____

_____

_____

_____

_____

_____

_____

Missing commas

Missing commas can also be confusing. For instance, read the following sentence:

> Mr. Alvario who was sick last year is in the hospital again.

Without commas, your reader will consider the "who" clause nonrestrictive, implying that there are several Mr. Alvarios to refer to. If there is no other Mr. Alvario, commas placed around the clause make your meaning clear:

> Mr. Alvario, who was sick last year, is in the hospital again.

The following sentence was written about the town dump by Wallace Stegner. With the commas left out, it is a very confusing sentence.

> But it had plenty of old iron furniture papers mattresses that were the delight of field mice and jugs and demijohns that were sometimes their bane for they crawled into the necks and drowned in the rainwater or redeye that was inside.

Originally, Stegner punctuated it carefully to clarify the items in a series and the two paralleled items that have restrictive clauses: the mattresses and the demijohns (very large bottles). The coordinating conjunction, "for," requires the usual comma before it. Note how much clearer the well-punctuated version is:

But it had plenty of old iron, furniture, papers, mattresses that were the delight of field mice, and jugs and demijohns that were sometimes their bane, for they crawled into the necks and drowned in the rainwater or redeye that was inside.

The semicolon in the following sentence by Judge Learned Hand is essential. Yet even if we keep it and leave out the commas, confusion reigns:

Ideas fashions dogmas literary political scientific and religious have a very similar course; they get a currency spread like wildfire have their day and thereafter nothing can revive them.

The commas in the original show that "fashions" and "dogmas" are modified by "literary, political, scientific, and religious." Consider the other confusions that are clarified:

Ideas, fashions, dogmas, literary, political, scientific, and religious, have a very similar course; they get a currency, spread like wildfire, have their day, and thereafter nothing can revive them.

In the following paragraph, all the commas are omitted. You may have to reread a sentence in order to understand its meaning and to punctuate it properly. (This will give you some insight into the effect your own comma errors have on your reader!) Note how the sentences can be read without a pause, causing you to read too fast for understanding. After you have read the paragraph, add commas where you think they are necessary; in each case, ask yourself *why* you are adding the comma. When you are finished, read the paragraph over, notice how much clearer it is with the proper commas and how the pauses they create help the meaning.

Wilson Walsh who sits next to me in math class is in despair. Having had so many things go wrong lately he can't think of anything to look forward to. He just sits there until Mr. Benoit our math teacher yells at him. Lately he doesn't even do his homework. When I try to talk with him he hears me but he doesn't listen. Not only is he lost in thought but he also seems to have given up on himself. Even his clothes which he used to wear carefully are mismatched and torn. His hair is several inches longer than usual and his shoes are a mess. Staring at Luisa the girl he used to date he sometimes seems close to tears. If he doesn't find something or someone to live for soon he may remain in despair or he may do something to hurt himself. I worry about him and I think his parents and teachers should be worried about him too.

Overuse of commas

As you have seen, commas are very helpful. They provide a pause that breaks up a long string of thoughts into small pieces of information. But if commas are overused, they can obscure the meaning of a sentence. Suppose you have written:

> The girl in the red-flowered dress, is my friend.

The comma after the word "dress" leads your reader to expect a clause or a phrase after it; he is forced to reread the sentence, taking out the comma, before he can make sense of it:

> The girl in the red-flowered dress is my friend.

It might help you to remember the following general rules:

1. A comma never separates a subject from its predicate verb.
2. A comma never separates a predicate verb from its object or complement.
3. A comma is not used before a conjunction coordinating two subjects, two predicates, or two phrases.

The paragraph below contains some commas that are properly used and some that are improperly used. Check each comma carefully; ask yourself whether there is a good reason for its being there. Rewrite the paragraph in the spaces provided, keeping the necessary commas and omitting those that interfere with the flow and meaning of the sentence.

> Until a few years ago, men, and women, did not live in the same dormitory. People thought, that such a living situation was improper. When co-ed dorms were first introduced, many questions were raised. Would women resent having men in the corridors, and in the rooms? Would it be possible for men and women to study, and to socialize under the same roof? Not all questions, have been answered. Unfortunately, some disturbing incidents have occurred, and some complaints have been registered. Still, having tried the experience, many dormitory residents, would have it no other way. They feel that men and women live, and work, very well together. Getting along with members of the opposite sex, is an important learning experience, for them. If universities tried to go back to the old dormitory system, these residents would protest vigorously. They would either write letters to the campus newspaper, or

put on a demonstration, and they might even threaten to leave the university.

_____

_____

_____

_____

_____

_____

_____

_____

_____

_____

_____

_____

Proofreading for sentence fragments

Sentence fragments are a continual problem for some beginning writers. The basic rule to remember is that every complete sentence must have a subject and a predicate verb. A review of Unit 6, "The Independent Clause," and Unit 7, "The Sentence Fragment," will be helpful at this point.

Proofreading for sentence fragments involves reading each sentence in a paragraph, checking to see that the sentence has a subject and a complete predicate verb. Be especially aware of subordinating conjunctions that make the following clause subordinate, not independent. Also be aware of the participle forms of the verb, which cannot be a predicate verb without a helper.

The following paragraph contains some complete sentences and some fragments. Underline each fragment and make sure that you know *why* it is a fragment. Then rewrite the paragraph in the spaces below. Change fragments to complete sentences using the techniques you learned in Unit 7.

Since Richard Nixon visited China, more and more people want to find out about that distant country. Aware of their lack of knowledge, because America had no trade relations with China for so many years. Some Americans planning to visit China in the next few years. This not altogether an easy task. Getting together the money. Special visas must still be obtained. Even if the planning goes well, travelers to China must anticipate a very long journey to get from the United States to the Chinese mainland. First they arrive at Hong Kong, and after a session telling them about Chinese customs, many of which are unfamiliar. Crossing the border, and accompanied by a Chinese interpreter. By American standards, hotel accommodations seem primitive. Nevertheless, the sights and sounds of China, the experience of meeting its people, the thrill of seeing famous landmarks such as the Great Wall or the Forbidden City in Peking. After their return, most people decide that it was worth the effort.

Proofreading the Sentence

Proofreading for run-on sentences

Continual problems with run-on sentences and overloaded sentences require a special strategy for correction. If you have these problems, you may be writing complete sentences, but joining too many of them together to make sense. One basic rule is to break down any long sentence in a paragraph into its component parts. (A review of Unit 8, "The Run-On Sentence" would be useful here.) Once you know how many independent clauses you have, and how many subordinate and modifying statements you have, you can proceed to punctuate the sentence properly. You may want to break the sentence up into two or more independent clauses so that its sense is clearer.

The following paragraph contains some run-on sentences and some overloaded sentences. Underline those sentences you think are faulty, then rewrite the paragraph in the spaces provided below. In the case of a comma splice, you may choose to join the independent clauses with a coordinating conjunction or with a semicolon, depending on the relationship between the clauses. In the case of overloaded sentences, you might create two shorter sentences. Whatever you do, your version of the paragraph should be free of run-on and overloaded sentences, but should retain complete independent clauses. Reread both paragraphs; your corrected version should be much clearer and its meaning should be more obvious to the reader.

Playing tennis with my friend Ruth is exciting she always makes it interesting. I never know what mood she will be in sometimes she is upset because of something that happened that day, angry, and she takes it out on me. Then I know that she will hit the ball as hard as she can, and she will even throw her racket in despair, narrowly missing me, if I'm anywhere near, which I usually am. If the ball is anywhere close the base line, she will call it out, which makes me mad, but there's nothing I can do about it. At other times, she will be in a silly mood, and I can expect a lot of joking around. When this happens, the game goes very slowly; I may even miss a shot because I'm laughing so hard. If she is feeling grim and serious, she plays by the book. I can almost see her mind going over how to hold the racket, how to place her feet, when to hit the ball, and where to place it. Then, there are no jokes, the game passes quickly. Sometimes she's in a good mood; she just wants to enjoy the game, playing the best she can. This provides the best game of all, for we both enjoy being out in the sun, exercising, and having a good time together.

_____

_____

_____

_____

_____

_____

_____

_____

_____

_____

Proofreading for wordiness

Wordiness is using more words than are necessary to express a thought. While not grammatically incorrect, wordy expressions tend to clutter a sentence, obscuring its meaning. Problems in this area fall into two general groups: empty words and phrases that must be completed by more concrete statements, and needless repetition.

Empty words and phrases often show up in rough drafts because the writer is putting off getting into the subject, or is having trouble with word choice. Some expressions to watch out for are listed below.

There is, there are, it is

These expressions mean little in themselves; furthermore, they put the subject, at the end of the sentence for no good reason. For example:

> It is very difficult to fly a kite in the rain.

"It is" adds nothing to the meaning of the sentence. The subject of the sentence is "to fly a kite in the rain." The idea can be expressed more forcefully by placing this subject first:

> Flying a kite in the rain is very difficult.

In the following example, an empty expression again puts off the main idea of the sentence:

> There is a major change taking place in American voting patterns.

This sentence can also be improved by placing the main idea first. Notice that this leads to changing the rather weak verb "is" to a more colorful verb, "are undergoing."

> American voting patterns are undergoing a major change.

Kind of, the fact that, the subject of

Some abstract nouns lead to wordiness. When you use these expressions, you are using an abstract noun that must be followed by another noun in order to have more complete meaning. Frequently, the abstract noun can simply be left out. For example:

I am going to write about <u>the subject of</u> women's rights today.

The expression "the subject of" adds no meaning to the sentence. The idea can be expressed more simply and forcefully:

I am going to write about women's rights today.

In the following sentence, the abstract expression adds clutter. Furthermore, it puts off the main idea of the sentence:

<u>The fact that</u> he has bad table manners doesn't bother me.

By leaving the abstract expression out, you can place the main idea first:

<u>His bad table manners</u> don't bother me.

The sentences below contain empty expressions. Underline these expressions and then rewrite the sentence in the space provided. Keep in mind that you want to place the main idea first and that you may want to change a form of the verb "to be" to a more concrete or colorful verb.

1. It is not always easy to teach a friend to dance.

_____

2. The fact that my friend Dwayne doesn't like to dance is annoying.

_____

3. He is the kind of person who would rather sit.

_____

4. The type of dancing I like best is ballroom dancing.

_____

5. When I start teaching Dwayne a lesson in ballroom dancing, he balks.

_____

6. There are other things he would rather be doing.

_____

Repetition can also cause wordiness since the same idea is being repeated twice, unnecessarily. Two main sources of repetition can be isolated:

Repeated parts of speech

Nouns are a particular problem here. Frequently, beginning writers repeat a noun or a noun plus a phrase, forgetting that they can either substitute a pronoun or leave the noun out entirely. For example:

> The people who work for state and federal government agencies receive many benefits. The employees of state and federal governments often have the benefit of job security. In addition, government employees have the benefit of medical insurance.

These sentences can be written more concisely by using the pronoun "they" for the phrase "the employees of state and federal governments" and by omitting the word "benefit" from all the sentences except the first. Notice that the latter leads to coordinating the nouns "job security" and "medical insurance":

> The people who work for state and federal government agencies receive many benefits. They often have job security and medical insurance.

Coordinated prepositional phrases and subordinate clauses can sometimes seem wordy if the same preposition or subordinating conjunction is repeated. In the following example the prepositional phrases are underlined:

> The President of the Bradford Little League gave awards to the coaches, to the umpires, and to the team managers.

The repeated "to the" can be left out:

> The President of the Bradford Little League gave awards to the coaches, umpires, and team managers.

Notice the repeated subordinating conjunctions in the following sentence. The subordinate clauses have been underlined for your convenience:

> After we find the man, after we secure his position, and
>
> after we give him the support he needs, we may begin to see
>
> the results we hoped for.

The repeated "after we" can be left out:

> After we find the man, secure his position, and give him the
>
> support he needs, we may begin to see the results we hoped for.

The above examples by no means cover all possibilities for repetition. If you have a problem in this area, keep the following basic idea in mind: any time you find yourself repeating a word or a phrase close to its initial use, ask yourself whether this repetition is strictly necessary to your meaning, or whether it enhances it in any way. If the answer is "no," try leaving the repetition out of the sentence, replacing it with a pronoun, or using some form of coordination.

Redundancy

This is a special kind of repetition. Here, two words meaning the same thing are used, or a second word is used whose meaning is already implicit in the first word. In either case, the second word can be left out. The redundancies are underlined in the following examples:

> She was a beautiful looking woman.
>
> He didn't know what time of day it was.
>
> Joan wore a red-colored dress.
>
> Mike understood the rules and regulations of driving.

In each of the above examples, the second word or phrase should be omitted:

> She was a beautiful woman.
>
> He didn't know what time it was.
>
> Joan wore a red dress.
>
> Mike understood the rules of driving.

The following exercise contains examples of wordiness caused by redundancy. Underline the word or words you think are redundant. Then write a more concise version of your own in the space provided.

1. The judge circled around the dogs at the show.

_____

2. Liz went to the movie. Ron went to the movie, too.

   _____

3. We will get our tickets when we have the money and when we have the
   time.

   _____

4. Mountain climbers are a special breed of people. These mountain climbers
   are special because they go places where others dare not follow.

   _____

   _____

5. The corporal advanced forward to a front-line position.

   _____

6. The special parking places are for handicapped people, for traffic police,
   and for reporters.

   _____

   _____

As we mentioned at the beginning of this chapter, you should learn to
recognize the errors you habitually make. Look over your recent writing and
decide what your most frequent editing problems are. Choose a sentence that
is typical of each of your usual problems. Then, in the space provided below,
write in: (1) the original sentence; (2) the type of error it contains (punctuation, sentence fragment, wordiness, and so on); and (3) the corrected
sentence.

_____

_____

SECTION V

Sentence Combining and Sentence Analysis

22   Combining Independent Clauses

Sentence combining is a technique that helps writers link short, choppy sentences together into one longer, more carefully structured sentence. Our approach to sentence combining depends on an understanding of those elements we have already studied: independent clauses, subordinate clauses, and all kinds of phrases. Thus anyone who has read the preceding units can grasp the principles and reap the benefits of sentence combining.

Let us begin by taking a pair of independent clauses and combining them into a single sentence. Each clause provides information that is essential to the finished sentence.

> Jasper and Rita want to learn the new algebra equations.
> Mr. Alvario wants to help Jasper and Rita.

One way to combine these independent clauses is:

> Mr. Alvario wants to help Jasper and Rita learn the new algebra equations.

This solution, while not the only one possible, is simple and clear. The most important point for you to note is that the finished sentence is, indeed, a combination of the two independent clauses.

Consider the following pairs of independent clauses and their combinations.

Independent clauses:	1. Mr. Alvario has set up a tutoring session right after school.
	2. Jasper and Rita have a softball game right after school.
Sentence combination:	Jasper and Rita's softball game conflicts with Mr. Alvario's tutoring session right after school.
Independent clauses:	1. Jasper is determined to go to the tutoring session.
	2. Rita is determined to play softball.
Sentence combination:	While Jasper plans to go to the tutoring session, Rita is determined to play softball.
Independent clauses:	1. Mr. Alvario wants Rita and Jasper to come to the tutoring session.
	2. Mr. Alvario will not force Rita and Jasper to come to the tutoring session.

Sentence combination: Although Mr. Alvario wants Rita and Jasper to
                         come to the tutoring session, he will not force them.

In the spaces provided below, write your own sentence combinations for
the pairs of independent clauses.

Independent clauses: 1. Rita and Jasper had an argument.
                        2. Rita and Jasper decided they would both go
                           either to tutoring or to softball.

Sentence combination: _____

                         _____

Independent clauses: 1. Rita argued very persuasively in favor of soft-
                           ball.
                        2. Jasper said he thought algebra was more im-
                           portant than softball.

Sentence combination: _____

                         _____

Independent clauses: 1. Rita said they could not let their team down.
                        2. Jasper said they could not let themselves down
                           by failing algebra.

Sentence combination: _____

                         _____

Continue and resolve Jasper and Rita's argument in the spaces below.
Write two short, independent clauses and then combine them into one longer
sentence.

Independent clauses: 1. _____

                         _____

2. _____

_____

Sentence combination: _____

_____

Independent clauses: 1. _____

_____

2. _____

_____

Sentence combination: _____

_____

Independent clauses: 1. _____

_____

2. _____

_____

Sentence combination: _____

_____

In the exercises above, you were combining only two independent clauses. But many sentences are combinations of three, four, five, and sometimes six independent clauses. Combining many independent clauses is not different in principle from combining two independent clauses. Examine the following combinations, then write your own sentence combinations in the spaces provided.

Independent clauses:
1. I am a new student in this school.
2. Darryl has been a student in this school for three years.
3. Darryl is acting as my guide in this school.

Sentence combination: Because I am a new student, Darryl, who has been in this school for three years, is acting as my guide.

Independent clauses:
1. Darryl is an honor student.
2. Darryl is the football captain.
3. Darryl has often been a guide for new students.

Sentence combination: Darryl, both an honor student and captain of the football team, often guides new students.

Independent clauses:
1. My first day in school was a bit frightening.
2. I did not know anyone in the school.
3. Darryl introduced me to dozens of students.

Sentence combination: My first day in school was a bit frightening because I did not know anyone, so Darryl introduced me to dozens of students.

Independent clauses:
1. Some students seemed a bit cool towards me.
2. Some students seemed very friendly.
3. I hope to make friends soon.

Sentence combination: Some students seemed very friendly, and some rather cool, but I hope to make friends soon.

Independent clauses:
1. Some of the courses in my new school are advanced.
2. Some of my new courses are easy.
3. I may have trouble getting caught up in all my new courses.

Sentence combination: _____

_____

_____

_____

Independent clauses: 1. English is an easy subject for me.
2. Mathematics is a moderately difficult subject for me.
3. Physics is the hardest subject I have ever taken.

Sentence combination: _____

_____

_____

_____

Independent clauses: 1. Mr. Alvario is my favorite teacher in my new school.
2. Mr. Alvario teaches algebra.
3. Algebra has never been my favorite subject.

Sentence combination: _____

_____

_____

_____

Independent clauses: 1. This year I may go out for a sport.
2. Basketball is the sport I play best.
3. The basketball team in my new school is terrific.

Sentence combination: _____

_____

_____

_____

In the following two exercises, provide three independent clauses and your sentence combination. Continue the narrative.

Independent clauses: 1. _____

_____

2. _____

_____

3. _____

_____

Sentence combination: _____

_____

_____

_____

Independent clauses: 1. _____

_____

2. _____

_____

3. _____

_____

Sentence combination: _____

_____

_____

_____

Combining two or three independent clauses into a single sentence is generally easy. As long as you make sure that all the clauses deal with the same, or a closely related, subject, you should not have difficulty. However, when more than three independent clauses are combined in a single sentence, the chances for loss of unity, clarity, and coherence are much greater when two to three statements are combined.

Below are groups of four independent clauses. Each group is followed by a single sentence formed by combining the clauses. The sentence, as it was published, is only one way of combining the independent clauses, but it is adequate to the writer's purpose and it is clear and complete.

The first sentence is from Martin Luther King's "Letter from Birmingham Jail":

Independent clauses: 1. I was confined in Birmingham city jail.
2. In jail I read your recent statement.
3. Your statement evaluates my present activities.
4. The evaluation calls my activities "unwise and untimely."

Sentence combination: While confined here in the Birmingham city jail, I came across your recent statement calling my present activities "unwise and untimely."

The following sentence is from an essay on greeting cards by Richard Rhodes:

Independent clauses: 1. There are schools of nursing.
2. There are schools of nuclear physics.
3. There are no schools of greeting cards.
4. Greeting-card makers become apprentices.

Sentence combination: There are schools of nursing and schools for nuclear physics, but there are no schools for the makers of greeting cards, only apprenticeships.

Lillian Hellman wrote the following sentence in her autobiography, *An Unfinished Woman*:

Independent clauses: 1. It was toward evening.
                        2. I moved to the French Quarter.
                        3. People were going home for dinner.
                        4. I was feeling sad and envious.

Sentence combination: Toward evening, I moved to the French Quarter,
                        feeling sad and envious as people went home for
                        dinner.

Complete the next two exercises. Each has four independent clauses
that must be joined to make a good sentence. In the space provided,
write your sentence combination. As a matter of strategy, decide which
| subject | + | predicate | structure in the four independent clauses is the
most important. Use this as the core of your sentence and use the rest of the
information in the other independent clauses to build around it. Use the
clauses and sentences above as models for this exercise

Independent clauses: 1. There are wonderful places in the world.
                        2. There is Nassau.
                        3. There is New York.
                        4. I prefer Chicago more than any other place.

Sentence combination: _____

                        _____

                        _____

Independent clauses: 1. Folklore is widespread.
                        2. Folklore is ancient.
                        3. The moon plays a prominent part in folklore.
                        4. The moon is supposed to drive people mad.

Sentence combination: _____

                        _____

                        _____

Independent clauses: 1. Basketball requires endurance.
                        2. Soccer requires agility.

3. Baseball requires speed.
4. Football requires endurance, agility, speed, and the capacity to withstand pain.

Sentence combination: _____

_____

_____

In the spaces provided below, write four independent clauses, then combine them into a single sentence. Be sure that each independent clause relates to a core subject around which you will build your final sentence.

Independent clauses:

1. _____

_____

2. _____

_____

3. _____

_____

4. _____

_____

Sentence combination: _____

_____

_____

_____

_____

In combining groups of short sentences, or independent clauses, into a single sentence, students often go astray and create a long involved sentence structure. Sentence analysis is a method of simplifying such an overcomplicated sentence. It helps clarify what is essential in the sentence and what is not, thereby permitting us to rewrite the sentence and make it clear.

In the following space, write one of your own long sentences that is overcomplicated and unclear.

Your own sentence: _____

_____

_____

_____

Now, in the spaces below, write the independent clauses that state everything you wanted to put into your combined sentence. Be sure to write everything in simple, direct statements.

Independent clauses: _____

_____

_____

_____

_____

_____

_____

Review each of the above independent clauses carefully. Find the $\boxed{\text{subject}}$ + $\boxed{\text{predicate}}$ structure around which you will build your sentence. After striking out any independent clauses that do not relate to your subject, combine the remaining clauses into a single long sentence. Compare this sentence to your original sentence. Your rewritten sentence, based on the combination of several short independent clauses, should be clear, concise, and uncomplicated.

Sentence combination: _____

_____

_____

_____

_____

23 Combining by Coordination and Subordination

If you can imagine that sentences are made up of short, independent clauses of the sort discussed in the preceding unit, you can then begin to see that combining statements into a sentence involves some basic decisions. You must spend some time analyzing the statements to decide which are roughly equal in value. Then you will coordinate roughly equal things, while subordinating those that seem less important.

Good writers usually put their most important idea in the independent clause of the sentence. If there is another very important idea that is just about equal to the first idea, a good writer will put it in a coordinate independent clause. If there is an idea or supporting condition that must be mentioned, but which is less immediately important, it can go in a subordinate clause or phrase. Good writers rarely put their most important ideas in subordinate structures.

Sentence combining: coordination

In the exercises that follow, a number of independent clauses are provided. Your job is to use the principles of coordination you learned in Section III and make one clear sentence from each group of statements. Remember, you may coordinate subjects, verbs, clauses, or phrases. The first example is done as a model of the process.

Independent clauses:
1. The Egyptians built temples.
2. The Greeks built temples.
3. The Romans built temples.
4. People worship gods in their temples.
5. People have celebrations in their temples.
6. People seek comfort in their temples.

Sentence combination: *The Egyptians, Greeks, and Romans built temples in which they worshiped their gods, held celebrations, and sought comfort.*

Independent clauses:
1. The college offers a degree in psychology.
2. It offers a degree in business science.
3. A student cannot get degrees in both areas.

Sentence combination: _____

_____

_____

Independent clauses:
1. Doctors see many sick people.
2. Some people have colds.
3. Some people have infections.
4. Some people have vague complaints.
5. Lawyers see many unhappy people.
6. Some people want divorces.
7. Some people are going bankrupt.
8. Some people have been cheated.

Sentence combination: _____

_____

_____

_____

Independent clauses: 1. On Mondays I eat in the kitchen.
                        2. I eat on the white porcelain table.
                        3. I eat fillet of flounder on Mondays.
                        4. On Wednesdays I eat in the dining room.
                        5. The mahogany table is in the dining room.
                        6. I only eat beef on the mahogany table.

Sentence combination: _____

                        _____

                        _____

Independent clauses: 1. Food is necessary to survival.
                        2. Fuel is necessary to survival.
                        3. Clothing is necessary to survival.
                        4. Things necessary to survival are in short supply.
                        5. Overpopulation threatens survival.
                        6. We have means to control overpopulation.

Sentence combination: _____

                        _____

                        _____

Sentence combining: subordination

The principles of subordination, discussed in detail in Section II, are basic to making sentences from independent clauses when some of the statements are much less significant than others. Of course, you are the person to decide just which statement will be "featured" in the independent clause and which will be given a "supporting role" in a subordinate clause or phrase. You should think of subordination as a means by which you can reflect your personal values.

Subordination, it is important to note, does not always imply inferiority or lack of importance. Very often, an idea that appears in a participial phrase or a subordinate clause will be crucial to understanding the sentence. This is particularly so if the subordinate element is at the beginning or the end of the sentence, since the reader is always struck most by the first or last structural element in a sentence.

Consider the following group of independent clauses. Using simple subordination, it is very simple to organize them into a single clear and coherent sentence:

1. Urbanization is a problem.
2. Industrialization is a problem.
3. Isolation is a problem.
4. Schools have helped cause these problems.
5. Schools have not helped solve these problems.

To make a useful and coherent sentence from those statements, we must examine the relationship between the two most important elements: the problems and the schools. Is there a relation of time, place, manner, condition, or cause between these elements that is implied in the statements? Well, as statement 4 suggests, there is a causal relation. Statement 5 seems to imply an "even though" condition. One way of making a sentence out of these statements would be to subordinate the schools' causing problems, and then to use the second part, the schools' solving the problems, in the main clause:

> Even though schools have helped create problems of urbanization, industrialization, and isolation, they have not helped solve them.

The three problems are coordinated as objects of the verb "helped create," (which is actually a verb, "helped," with an infinitive "to create" used without its sign "to." This is common in English. The three problems are still objects, but actually objects of the infinitive.) The subordinator, "Even though," sets up expectations in the sentence. These expectations are not clarified until the independent clause: "they have not helped solve them." There are many ways to write this particular sentence, and you might have a better idea yourself. Examine the next examples for opportunities to subordinate structures within sentences. Consider questions of time, place, manner, condition, cause, and any other qualifiers of action.

Independent clauses: 1. Mr. Alvario came home early.
2. The TV was on by mistake.
3. He saw himself interviewed on the news.
4. He did not expect the interview to be on until much later.

Sentence combination: _____

_____

_____

Independent clauses:
1. Robert Kennedy was dedicated to civil rights.
2. Civil-rights laws angered many people.
3. Kennedy spoke out on civil rights anyway.

Sentence combination: _____

_____

_____

Independent clauses:
1. People are worried about getting jobs.
2. Jobs are scarce.
3. Good jobs are even scarcer.
4. College degrees do not guarantee jobs.
5. Some people who want jobs do not go to college.

Sentence combination: _____

_____

_____

Independent clauses:
1. Jobs are very scarce.
2. Colleges provide good education.
3. Colleges do not provide jobs.
4. Students still want an education.

Sentence combination: _____

_____

_____

Independent clauses: 1. Fishing is a sport.
                                             2. It is not like tennis.
                                             3. Tennis requires running around after a ball.
                                             4. Fishing requires concentration.
                                             5. Fishermen concentrate on the stream.
                                             6. They concentrate on the fish.
                                             7. Tennis players concentrate on the ball and the racquet.
                                             8. Some tennis players do not think fishing is a sport.

Sentence combination: _____

_____

_____

Sentence combining is valuable for helping you rewrite sentences that may have given you problems. Analyzing a problem sentence for chances to subordinate and coordinate important elements is one of the best means of improving your writing. Take this opportunity to find a problem sentence in your own writing. Write the sentence below, then list the brief statements you wanted to put in your sentence. Add any you feel were left out. Then rewrite the sentence. Was your most useful principle subordination? Coordination? Both?

Your own sentence: _____

_____

_____

_____

Statements (you may have more or less than six):

1. _____

2. _____

3. _____

4. _____

5. _____

6. _____

Sentence rewritten: _____

_____

_____

_____

24 Inventing Models

Sometimes it is necessary to simplify your writing. Many writers tend toward an overcomplicated style and don't realize how they might be more direct. One way is to pay close attention to the structure of sentences in any passage you write. Most professional writers aim for variety in their sentences, but they also aim for clarity and precision. Clarity is often achieved by writing very direct, often short, sentences that begin with the subject of the sentence. Precision is often achieved by careful coordination or subordination or both. By explaining something in brief sentences, the writer can make each point clearly enough for the reader to contemplate it. By means of subordination, the elements of time, cause, comparison, condition, place, and action can all have their turn to clarify the subject of the sentence. By use of coordination, similar elements can be drawn into the discussion as a means of emphasizing and clarifying the main point.

Most writers eventually come to understand the points raised above, but they have a hard time actually putting those points into practice. Professional writers prefer short sentences. They like to have their subject right up front where the reader can see it. Only after the reader is thoroughly acquainted with the writer and his or her material will longer and more complex sentences begin to show up. When they do, the reader is usually prepared for them. Student writing is not professional writing, but that does not mean a student cannot learn from looking at a professional's prose. Directness, simplicity, and clarity are valuable in any kind of prose. Controlling the structure of sentences in a passage is also valuable in any kind of prose. Too much sameness dulls the reader; variety is just as essential as imagination in writing.

The following problems are actually exercises designed to help sharpen your attention toward sentence structure. Your repertoire of sentence elements, of the basic parts and the basic approaches to arranging those parts is advanced enough so that such exercises can be enormously valuable. They can help you see the usefulness of what you have learned as well as give you a sense of the extent of what you have learned. When you are working on these exercises, remember that it is the spirit of them that counts and not the letter. Should you be unable to do exactly what is asked for, try your best to come as close as possible. Even coming close will teach you a great deal about sentence patterning and sentence variety.

Using the independent clause: IC

You have had plenty of practice with the independent clause. However, you should realize that many writers can produce lengthy prose made up of nothing but a string of sentences that are only independent clauses. It is not necessarily desirable to make all your sentences such simple structures; but it is essential that you be able to make some of them that simple. And you should be careful to be sure your *real* subject, the main topic or idea, is the subject of your sentence. That may sound silly on the surface, but it is not. Many writers put their *real* subject in a prepositional phrase or use it as the object or complement of the verb. This is unwise. The natural focal point of the subject of the predicate verb is usually best for your *real* subject.

For the purposes of the following exercise, use this basic pattern for your sentences: subject + predicate verb. You may add as many adverbial, adjectival, and phrase modifiers as you like. This means you may string a group of prepositional phrases before the subject, after it, or after the predicate verb. You may also use participial phrases, gerund phrases, or infinitive phrases. The point is that your basic sentences should be independent clauses. Limit the modifiers to phrases in this exercise.

Examine the first example, then do the exercise that follows it.

> Making good photographs is not easy. Along with questions of light, questions of space, and questions relating to the technical capacities of the camera and the film, the photographer has to deal with questions of aesthetics. Aesthetics pertains to the artistic qualities of the finished photograph. The only sure way of grasping and understanding the aesthetics of the photograph

is by means of study. The history of photography is the first thing for the photographer to study. Only by studying closely the achievements of great photographers can anyone hope to produce a full, imaginative, and satisfying photograph. Without that study, most of us can only hope to produce work influenced by a limited amount of probably recent photos from newspapers, magazines, or shows in our immediate vicinity. That is good enough for many photographers. But for really deep, serious, and committed photographers it is not enough. Only the most thorough understanding of the achievements of the medium will do for the best photographers. Without that understanding, most photographers are little more than technicians. They manipulate their f/stops and their light-emitting diode readouts. They manipulate their development time. They manipulate their paper. But they do not make photographs. They make forgettable images.

The passage above is written entirely in sentences made up of nothing more complex than an independent clause. The tedium of that simple structure is relieved by the use of participial, infinitive, prepositional, and gerund phrases. Sometimes a string of phrases is used, as in the second sentence, which uses parallel structure: paralleling "questions of" three times before the subject and once after it. The use of various kinds of phrases within those parallelisms is really very natural to most of us. You have had considerable practice with such structures earlier in this book. Here is a chance to put them together in a controlled essay. Your job is to:

1. write a brief essay using sentences that have no more than one independent clause
2. use as many phrases as you like
3. aim for a variety of long and short sentences

You may choose your own subject. Should you not have a subject, choose from the following.

1. Describe how the energy crisis has affected you or people you know.
2. What kind of car should someone buy today?
3. Which television series best represents real life experiences? Give examples.

Your essay: _____

_____

_____

_____

_____

_____

_____

_____

_____

_____

_____

_____

_____

_____

Mixing independent clauses: IC + IC

Another very often used structure for sentences is the following:

| independent clause | + | coordinating conjunction | + | independent clause |

It would be very difficult to write a passage that uses nothing but this pattern since the reader would soon crave variety. You must season such a passage with a brief sentence of a single independent clause, as in the exercise on pages 148–49. Consequently, examine the following passage, which uses a great many sentences of the IC + IC pattern. It also breaks that pattern with brief sentences of the single IC pattern. Again, use as many phrases as possible in order to say all that there is to be said.

> Television and movies love heroes, but their heroes are not always people. James Bond movies are adventure films and they ought to have a truly adventurous hero doing truly adventurous things. And they do. But we also notice the screen time is shared with another hero in those films, and that hero is often the automobile designed for our spy, Mr. Bond. It has special armor and bulletproof glass, and it has a sleek, feline, deft, even sexy, design according to some viewers. Not only does the Aston-Martin DB-9 excite Mr. Bond from his very first inspection onward, but it also seems to excite the audiences crowding the movie theaters here and abroad. Sometimes the real hero of the film seems to be the car itself. Movies rerun often on television are, like the 007 mysteries, adventure films, and they hardly ever miss the chance to feature a high-speed car race. *Bullitt* and *The French Connection* have two of the best car-chase sequences, and, how, with all that squealing, roaring action, can flesh-and-blood mortal heroes compete with such immortal machines? Maybe they don't. Maybe the real heroes of those films are the cars, and maybe we are the real drivers of those cars (in our imagination, of course).

Your job in the following is to:

1. write a brief essay using mainly the pattern of

| independent clause | + | independent clause |

2. use some sentences with only one independent clause as a means of gaining variety
3. use as many phrases as you like

You may choose your own subject. Should you not have a subject, choose from the following.

1. Do the men you know treat women as equals?
2. Which house or apartment that you have lived in did you like best?
3. Explain why you would prefer owning one item in the following list rather than the other items: a boat, a seaplane, an island, a raft, water skis, a surfboard.

Your essay: _____

_____

_____

_____

_____

_____

_____

_____

_____

_____

_____

_____

_____

_____

_____

_____

Mixing independent clauses and subordinate clauses: IC + IC + SC

As we have seen in our earlier work with subordination, there are many ways of including a subordinate clause in a sentence. We should examine some of the most useful patterns. In the following list, IC stands for independent clause, while SC stands for subordinate clause. These are not the *only* patterns a writer can use. Indeed, the patterns available to a writer are virtually without number. Rather, these are the most obvious, the simplest, and possibly the most useful patterns at the writer's disposal:

1. SC + IC.
2. IC + SC.
3. SC + IC + IC.
4. IC + IC + SC.
5. SC + SC + IC.
6. IC + SC + SC.
7. I(SC)C.
8. IC + I(SC)C + SC.

The patterns are endless, and these may help you see some of the alternatives from which you may draw. The following example is drawn from these alternatives. All the sentences rely on the clarifications of time, place, action, condition, description, and cause. *There are eight sentences in the following paragraph. They follow the order of the eight models set up above.*

Although not everyone can have a chance, acting in the college drama productions is really valuable. Great politicians have often begun their careers in a political play like *Henry V* when they discover they enjoy being the king. After they get a taste of power, they set about studying it more closely, and the best study of power is the use of it in practice. Politicians benefit from their student drama days, and so do teachers, whose performances in class sometimes seem a bit theatrical. Because the actor gains poise, and because the drama explores real life situations, being in a play can be the most important learning experience of a college student. The right play can give someone a push in a professional direction, particularly if that person was heading there in the first place, or if that person has a special skill brought to light in the play. The student actors who get the chance can make very practical use of their playing days. Dramatic experience could realistically be required, and plays that use legions of actors could be produced in open air theaters; consequently everyone could have a chance.

This exercise is not as difficult as you might at first assume. Your job in the space below is to write a brief essay that uses a variety of subordinate clauses linked to independent clauses in your sentences. Ideally, it would be useful for you to try to do what was done in the example and follow the sentence patterns listed before the passage. You need not follow the same order of patterns; you may want to mix them up. If you do, explain what your order is in the space provided.

You may choose your own subject or choose from the following.

1. Are people's moods really governed by the weather?
2. What were the most important courses your high school offered?
3. Choose the best means of travel from the following group, and compare it with the others: car, train, steamship, plane, bus, bicycle, motorcycle, skateboard.

Your sentence patterns: 1. _____   2. _____

3. _____   4. _____   5. _____   6. _____

7. _____   8. _____

Your essay: _____

_____

_____

_____

_____

_____

_____

_____

_____

_____

_____

_____

_____

_____

25 Learning from Professional Writers

As we mentioned earlier, student prose is not professional prose, and, happily, never has to be measured against it. But the writer who is successful with his or her prose is doing something that all of us can learn from. However, not all instructors agree that writing can be learned from looking at professional work, and you may agree with them. But the exercises here may help you learn something fundamental about the way sentences are combined into paragraphs. They may help you see that the choices available to the professional writer are also available to you. We can learn a great deal about writing from looking closely at the sentences in professional prose.

The first part of the exercises that follow involves analyzing the structure of sentences according to the patterns we used in the last chapter (page 153). We are interested in noting the independent clauses and the subordinate clauses. To be sure, each sentence we look at will have phrases of various kinds, but we will not analyze them for these phrases since we are trying to learn something about the *basic* structure of the sentences. Where specially paralleled phrases appear, we will note them because they can contribute to the special stylistic achievement of a given passage.

The second part of the exercises involves using the same pattern of sentences the professional writer has used. You are not to imitate the professional's style or tone. It is almost impossible to do this, anyway. Instead, you are to see if, by following the example of the professional, your own writing sounds more professional.

EXERCISE 1

The first example shows both parts of the exercise: an essay by Lewis Mumford is analyzed for its sentence structure, and then used as the basis for an original essay.

Where did the machine first take form in modern civilization? There was plainly more than one point of origin. Our mechanical civilization represents the convergence of numerous habits, ideas, and modes of living, as well as technical instruments; and some of these were, in the beginning, directly opposed to the civilization they helped to create. But the first manifestation of the new order took place in the general picture of the world: during the first seven centuries of the machine's existence the categories of time and space underwent an extraordinary change, and no aspect of life was left untouched by this transformation.

Sentence patterns: 1. IC
2. IC
3. IC + IC + SC
4. IC + SC + IC

Essay built from Mumford's pattern

How have we been able to afford the world's most extensive highway system? Careful taxation of gasoline was the most important first step. Our highways are the result of many kinds of taxation, however; some of them involve taxing trucks and commercial vehicles in addition to those vehicles that use the roads for pleasure. But the most important step after taxation was the formation of the Highway Building Fund: during its several decades of existence it was never used for anything but building highways, and the laws protecting the fund guaranteed us millions of miles of the most enviable highways in the history of the world.

You have read Mumford's essay and examined the essay built from Mumford's pattern. Take the same sentence patterns and write your own essay below. Choose a subject of your own, or write about one of the following: working, a sport you enjoy, the kind of job you'd like after college, or a person who annoys you.

Your essay: _____

_____

_____

_____

_____

_____

_____

_____

_____

_____

_____

EXERCISE 2

The following passage is from a short story by Ann Petry.

> She frightened me. She had frightened Pedro, too; he was pale
> and his eyes looked bigger. I had thought my father was late
> for dinner because he had stopped somewhere to talk and got
> involved in a long-winded conversation, and that if Pedro and I
> had walked up or down the street we would have found him
> and told him his dinner was ready. Aunt Sophronia obviously
> thought something dreadful had happened to him. Now we
> began to think so, too.

Sentence patterns: 1. IC
                         2. IC + IC + IC
                         3. IC + SC + SC + SC + IC + IC
                         4. IC + SC
                         5. IC

You will see that although the sentences look simple, they are very
complex structures. They are functional because they have short independent
units. Study the passage and the sentence patterns. Then write your own
description of a fictional situation using the same pattern of sentences Petry
uses.

Your essay: _____

_____

_____

_____

_____

_____

_____

_____

_____

EXERCISE 3

The following is from an article by Leonard A. Stevens.

> A unique festival is now held each June in Santee, California. It features a long, colorful Saturday morning parade that starts from a shopping center and ends at the town's sewage treatment plant. For the remainder of the weekend, as many as ten thousand people celebrate the recent construction of five beautiful man-made lakes laid out in a line for the better part of a mile. At this "Festival of the Lakes," people fish, picnic, boat and swim, with little concern that nearly every drop of the water is supplied by Santee's municipal sewage system.

Sentence patterns: 1. _____ 2. _____ 3. _____

4. _____

Write your own descriptive essay using the sentence patterns you wrote out.

Your essay: _____

_____

_____

_____

_____

_____

_____

_____

_____

_____

EXERCISE 4

The following is from an essay by Igor Kon.

> The adolescent must make choices in every sphere of life. He
> must choose his occupation. He must choose his mate. He must
> decide what his ethical beliefs are, how he will live, etc. The
> process is a hard one and engenders the doubts and vacillations
> so typical of adolescence. Characteristically, it is at this age
> that the meaning of life becomes so important. The adolescent

is searching for some formula that will explain his reason for being and give him direction. Where can he get this formula?

Sentence patterns: 1. _____ 2. _____ 3. _____

4. _____ 5. _____ 6. _____ 7. _____

Write your own essay based on this pattern of sentences.

Your essay: _____

_____

_____

_____

_____

_____

_____

_____

_____

_____

_____

_____

_____

EXERCISE 5

Find a brief paragraph by a modern writer you respect. Study the passage carefully and write its patterning of sentences.

Sentence patterns: 1. _____   2. _____   3. _____

4. _____   5. _____   6. _____   7. _____

8. _____   9. _____

Write your own essay using the very same pattern of sentences.

Your essay: _____

_____

_____

_____

_____

_____

_____

_____

_____

_____

Proofreading the Paragraph

26 Unity

The sentences in one paragraph usually have a single topic or idea. When they do, the paragraph is said to have unity, or oneness. This is not to say that every sentence deals with exactly the same subject, nor does it mean that every sentence uses a variant of the same predicate verb. What it means is that each sentence in the paragraph deals with the same general idea and that every subsequent sentence carries that idea a bit further. Like the sentence, the paragraph is a unit. The sentence can be un-unified just as the paragraph can be un-unfied. If the sentence wanders off into subsidiary issues and loses track of its subject, it loses unity. Unity may also be lost if the material discussed in subordinate clauses differs entirely from that in the independent clause.

Unity in the sentence

Achieving unity in the sentence is much easier when you know the basic parts of the sentence and how they are joined. Our previous work in subordination, coordination, and in sentence combining and analysis is designed to help you achieve unity in sentences. As a guide to proofreading for unity, consider the following points.

Proofreading for sentence unity:

1. Is the subject of the independent clause clear?
2. Do the subordinate clauses relate to that subject directly?
3. Do all the subordinate phrases help clarify the subject?
4. Has secondary subject matter been carefully related to the primary subject?

Overloading is probably the greatest single cause of loss of unity in a sentence. We have already discussed this problem in Section I, Unit 8. But it is worth noting that your chances of wandering from your subject without realizing it are greatest in sentences that simply become too long. Sometimes overlong sentences seem almost to have been written in two parts, and at two different sittings. Every long sentence should be proofread carefully for unity.

Let us begin by considering an actual sentence written by a student in an essay.

> Also my mother is a very hard worker, who is as very much a supporting crutch as my father.

Taking our four proofreading questions in turn, we find that, (1), the subject of the independent clause is clear. It is the fact that "my mother is a very hard worker." But, for (2), "Do the subordinate clauses relate to that subject directly?" we must answer, "No." We cannot be sure how the mother's being a supporting crutch is related to her being a hard worker. In fact, the "who" clause is not even clearly related to "worker." It is a restrictive clause (see Unit 12, pointer on page 70), but the writer, using a comma, makes it a nonrestrictive clause, which causes confusion. The answer to (3) is also "No." as is the answer to (4). In this sentence, the writer has failed to subordinate correctly, and the sentence has lost its unity. There are two subjects here: my mother is a hard worker; my mother is a supporting crutch.

How can this problem be solved? There are actually many ways to solve it. Let us begin by using the methods we discussed in Units 21 and 22: sentence combining. The first step is to find the independent clauses in the sentence.

Independent Clauses: 1. My mother is a very hard worker.
2. My father is a very hard worker.
3. My mother is a supporting crutch.
4. My father is a supporting crutch.

We can see that the solution to making this sentence unified lies in using careful coordination. This analysis clearly shows that the mother and the father have two qualities in common, both of which can be easily coordinated with the other. We can correct this sentence and improve its unity in many ways. Examine these different ways listed below.

1. My mother and father are hard workers and supporting crutches.
2. Not only are my mother and father hard workers, they are also like supporting crutches.
3. My father and mother are hard workers; they are also like supporting crutches.

You may feel the original sentence is not very good to start with, ending as it does with a metaphor that is not entirely clear. But the writer really wants to say two things about his parents, and with some patience and good proofreading, he can achieve unity. It would be easier, to be sure, if the writer were to talk about something other than supporting crutches. But even with that concept, the writer can make the sentence work.

Examine the next three sentences and offer your own corrections. Be prepared to offer appropriate answers to the proofreading questions on page 165. Spaces are provided for you to write the independent clauses.

1. The worst part of taking out the garbage is that if you use paper bags like we do, they leak and many times I have had to change my pants just before a date.

Independent clauses: 1. _____

2. _____

3. _____

4. _____

5. _____

6. _____

Your correction: _____

_____

_____

2. Fred appears in another situation where he is seen in a market, there a customer takes for granted that he is one of the employees.

Independent clauses: 1. _____

2. _____

3. _____

4. _____

Your correction: _____

_____

_____

3. Can uncertainty remind us of the frequent moments in our own lives when we are faced with difficult decisions or forced to endure long periods of silence while waiting to hear whether or not a loved one has survived a serious operation?

Independent clauses: 1. _____

2. _____

3. _____

4. _____

5. _____

Your correction: _____

_____

_____

Unity in the paragraph

The same principles that hold for unity in a sentence hold for unity in a paragraph. The paragraph, with its single topic, with sentences that develop that topic, and with a careful ordering of secondary subject matter, can hope to achieve a unity as strong as that of a good sentence. We can ask questions of the paragraph, as we did of the sentence, in order to decide on its unity.

Proofreading for paragraph unity:

1. Has the overall topic been stated clearly?
2. Does each sentence in the paragraph relate clearly to that topic?
3. Are sub-topics closely related to the main topic?
4. Do the sub-topics remain clearly subordinate to the main topic of the paragraph?

The following sample paragraph is from an essay in *Time*. Its overall topic is stated in the first sentence of the paragraph. Examine it and answer the rest of the questions on proofreading for paragraph unity.

1. Crime in the U.S. is a national disgrace. Police blotters are mired in the petty misdeeds of shoplifters and purse snatchers; courts are clogged with the violent felonies of rapists and murderers. By any standard of measurement, the statistics are staggering, and their impact can be felt at every level of

American life. One boy in every six will turn up in a juvenile court for a nontraffic offense before he is 18. In some urban areas, nearly half of all the residents stay off the streets at night for fear of attack, a third have grown too cautious to speak to strangers, a fifth have become so terrified that they would prefer to move out of their present neighborhoods. More and more people report that they keep firearms at home for self-protection; watchdogs are becoming as popular as the friendly family pet. There is a growing tendency to believe that the Government cannot or will not protect the average citizen.

This paragraph achieves unity by making sure that all its elements relate back to the opening sentence. Not every paragraph will do this. Some will achieve unity by having each sentence include an idea that will relate to the main idea of the paragraph yet may never be stated so clearly as is done in this example. If you go back to the four questions we asked, you will see that the answer to all of them is clearly "Yes." The topic is clear; each sentence is clearly related to it, as are the sub-topics—particularly the last, the fear that government may not be able to protect the average citizen.

Consider paragraph 2. There is a subject, but it is very much lost in the meanderings of the writer. After you have read the paragraph, ask the four questions above. Then write the main topic and the several sub-topics on the lines provided. This is equivalent to listing the independent clauses used for sentence combining.

▶ **POINTER FOR PROOFREADING PARAGRAPHS**

When proofreading these paragraphs for unity, you will also find it essential to proofread for punctuation, agreement, fragments, run-ons, and wordiness. Your job is not just to take the existent sentences and rearrange them. It is to make these paragraphs a-chieve unity and to turn them into good writing. You will need to do considerable rewriting.

---

2. Usually the average income that a person makes per year depends on their occupation, but in the 1976 Gallup Opinion Index, the percentage in favor of the capital punishment law differs with the highest income and the best occupation which seems unusual according to the middle to high income persons, the percentage of changed opinions since 1972 has been the closest to the manual workers. Usually you would see the high income persons with the professional occupations. People in the highest income bracket are of a high percentage in favor of the

death penalty probably because they don't care if they suffer before the criminals are killed, as long as they have their money. On the other hand, their occupations are affected, as well as their standards of life. Professional businessmen would like the convicted person to suffer for their wrongs. Even if convicts are put in jail for life, they could be up for parole in twenty-five years of so. If the person has definitely murdered someone, they should pay for it and be killed also. But if the person wants to be killed, he should have to suffer in jail.

This paragraph is a sample from student prose. You may not agree with its sentiments, and you may not wish to include all the sub-topics in your revision. Indeed, the first step to achieving unity is to separate the sub-topics relevant to the main topic into two categories: those that will aid unity and those that will not aid unity and should be discarded.

The main topic of the paragraph: _____

_____

List of sub-topics that aid unity: _____

_____

_____

List of sub-topics that do not aid unity and should be discarded: _____

_____

_____

_____

Your revision (aimed at greater unity): _____

_____

_____

The next example is also from student prose, but the difficulties are not quite so great. The writer is relatively close to finding the central topic, although it is not stated as clearly or effectively as it might be. It is likely that you will have less work revising this paragraph than the previous one.

3. Marriage is a difficult institution. This difficulty becomes compounded when the partners are from different socioeconomic backgrounds. People who are raised to value different ideas toward economic and social matters will continue to view these things from their own standpoint once they have entered into marriage. Some kind of accordance on these issues is necessary unless one partner is to be totally subservient to the other. Although it may be possible to make adjustments, it is unlikely that one's values will change drastically. It can be shown, statistically, that marriages among people of different socioeconomic backgrounds have a higher failure rate than those from a similar one. People from different backgrounds have few things in common. Their preferences in social activity and literature might differ which would serve to create a gap in the relationship. Marriage consists of a series of shared goals which are influenced by the values that each person brings into the relationship. What becomes of these goals when the values they are derived from are incongruent?

The main topic of the paragraph: _____

_____

List of sub-topics that aid unity: _____

_____

_____

List of sub-topics that do not aid unity and should be discarded: _____

_____

_____

Your revision (aimed at greater unity): _____

_____

_____

_____

_____

_____

_____

_____

27 Coherence

"Coherence" refers to continuity and to logical relationships among the sentences in a paragraph. Of course, you should always check to make sure that the subject of your paragraph has been developed through a logical sequence. But sometimes a paragraph may inherently possess continuity, yet not seem immediately clear to your reader. You can use special techniques to emphasize coherence, helping your reader to follow the flow of your paragraph development and giving him guideposts so that he does not have to reread the passage in order to understand your meaning.

Parallel sentence structure and repetition of key words

This technique uses two forms of repetition effectively to keep the main subject or attitude of your paragraph clearly in the reader's mind. It should be used judiciously, and is especially useful when you are developing a complicated idea. The following short paragraph illustrates how it is done:

> My brother's classmates are not always kind. They often ridicule each other, making fun of the weaknesses they know so well. They use physical abuse, hitting and tripping and throwing any available object. These seventh graders should know better, since they themselves are often the butt of jokes. Nevertheless, they continue to play tricks and call each other names, creating a tense atmosphere in the classroom.

Several kinds of repetition have been used here. All the sentences follow the basic sentence pattern  ; furthermore, the subject is always some form of reference to the classmates, making them the main focus of the paragraph. These two repetitions, sentence pattern and subject, keep the reader's mind focused on the main idea.

The repetition of key words takes special skills, since merely repeating the same word would lead to wordiness. Three main methods of repeating the same idea in different ways were used in the above paragraph:

1. *Synonyms*, such as the word "seventh graders" for "classmates."
2. *Pronouns*, such as "they" for "classmates."
3. *Pronominal adjectives*, such as "these" in "these seventh graders."

The paragraph below does not use any of the techniques discussed to develop coherence. Read the paragraph carefully, then decide what you want its main focus to be. Then rewrite the sentences in the space provided, using parallel sentence structure and key word repetition for greater coherence.

> Old age homes need not be gloomy, depressing places. Communal activities can bring residents together, helping them form friendships and share experiences. Daily meals are something to look forward to, if the cooks prepare food carefully and use their imagination to make each meal appealing. Visitors from the community should be encouraged. Morale can improve with bright, cheerful surroundings. Many residents respond well to simple concern for cleanliness and attentiveness to their needs on the part of nurses and aides.

_____

_____

_____

_____

_____

_____

_____

Conjunctive adverbs and special adjectives: transition

These words serve as transitions pointing to the logical relationships you are developing in your paragraph. They are often placed at the beginning of a sentence, indicating the relationship between that sentence and the previous one. However, they may be placed within the sentence as well.

Following is a list of frequently used conjunctive adverbs. You may find others in your own writing or in your reading.

1. *Order*: first (second, third), next, furthermore, in addition, moreover, also, last, in conclusion, finally
2. *Cause and effect*: as a result, consequently, hence, thus, therefore
3. *Contrast*: nevertheless, however, on the other hand, still

The conjunctive adverbs are underlined in the examples below. Notice how they clarify the logical relationship between the two sentences. Read the sentences again without the conjunctive adverb. In each case, the logical sequence becomes unclear.

1. Our high school coach had a good personality. Furthermore, he led our team on to a winning season.
2. The administration's policies for energy conservation were well intentioned. However, they failed for lack of support.
3. The food in the cafeteria is often cold, and it is relatively expensive. Therefore, few students eat there.

Some adjectives also help to establish logical relationships between sentences. They may be the same words as those listed above, although used as adjectives rather than as conjunctive adverbs. Other adjectives are entirely different. A partial list follows.

1. *Order*: first, next, other, another, additional, similar, last, final
2. *Cause and effect*: resulting, consequent, ensuing, following
3. *Contrast*: different, opposite, contrasting, contrary

The special adjectives are underlined in the following examples. Like conjunctive adverbs, they provide continuity and logic for the ideas expressed in the two sentences.

1. The mothers complained that the time needed to run their homes kept them from getting a job. Another factor was the lack of day care centers.
2. Principal MacIntyre announced that all lunch-time privileges were suspended until further notice. The ensuing uproar nearly overwhelmed him.

3. The <u>first</u> speaker proposed that anyone littering the highways should be fined. His opponent took a <u>different</u> position, suggesting that litterers should be put in jail.

In the following paragraph, underline the conjunctive adverbs and the special adjectives used to develop coherence.

Graduation from high school can be a confusing occasion. On the one hand, it can be a time for celebration. Graduates are usually glad to have finished four years of high school successfully. In addition, they may be looking forward to their plans for the future, whether they intend to work or to go on to school somewhere. The presence of relatives and friends at the graduation ceremony is another source of excitement. On the other hand, it is a time of sadness and uncertainty as well. As graduating seniors look around them, they realize that they may never see some of their classmates again. As a result, they may feel nostalgic about the experiences they have shared with them. Furthermore, the future is an unknown, less secure perhaps than the years spent in high school. Finally, parents may feel a twinge of regret as they realize that their children are growing up and leaving home. In sum, graduation is a time of change: a marker of endings and beginnings, creating mixed feelings for all concerned.

The following paragraph does not contain any special words to enhance coherence. Read the paragraph carefully, paying careful attention to the logical relationship between sentences. You may have to reread in order to ascertain what that relationship is. Then rewrite the paragraph in the space provided below, using conjunctive adverbs, subordinating conjunctions, and special adjectives where they are necessary or helpful in clarifying the development of the subject. Underline the words you have added.

Maintaining long-distance friendships requires special effort. The people involved have usually been used to seeing each other often. This is how the friendship probably developed. One person moves away. They both have to decide how to keep in touch. They may write letters to each other. One person may not be a very good correspondent. They stop writing as time goes on. Phone calls are a possible means of communication. They can get too expensive. Visits back and forth may help the relationship to continue. Transportation can be expensive, whether it is by car, bus, train, or air. The friends may decide that the expense isn't worth it, or they may simply be unable to afford it. If two people make the effort, they may be able to sustain and even develop the friendship they began with. Long distance friendship is never quite the same as being able to see a friend easily and often.

_____

_____

_____

_____

_____

_____

_____

_____

_____

In your own recent writing, find a paragraph whose coherence can be improved. First, read the paragraph over to be sure that you have developed the subject in a logical fashion. You may want to change the sentence order you previously used. Then consider what the logical relationship between sentences in the paragraph is and decide what method would best clarify that relationship. Rewrite the paragraph in the space below using parallel sentence structure, repetition of key words, conjunctive adverbs, and special adjectives to enhance coherence and help your reader follow the logical sequence of the paragraph. Underline the words you have used to bring this about.

_____

_____

_____

_____

_____

_____

_____

_____

_____

_____

SECTION VII

Tests
and
Evaluations

Diagnostic Test

A. General Usage   Read each of the following sentences over carefully. If the sentence is correct as it stands, put a *C* beside it in the space provided. If you find an error in the sentence, circle the error and rewrite the sentence correctly on the line provided after each sentence.

_____   1. His habitual custom was to jog every morning.

_____

_____   2. The excited children jumped up and down in their seats they cheered noisily.

_____

_____   3. Because we watched television so much, we grew up to be observers, not participants.

_____

_____   4. I enjoyed playing football, running around the track, and was especially fond of tennis.

_____

_____   5. The director of the school showing a way to explain science to the children.

_____

_____ 6. The students in the parking lot is gesturing wildly.

_____

_____ 7. Reggie Jackson who made a record number of home runs has had a candy bar named after him.

_____

_____ 8. Driving to school, my car got a flat tire.

_____

_____ 9. Because of the fact that I like ice cream, I go to the soda shop every day.

_____

_____ 10. Everybody in the play is going to enjoy the cast party after the performance.

_____

_____ 11. When you return to your dorms after this morning's class you will receive your mail.

_____

_____ 12. Darlene wasn't suppose to receive your money; I was.

_____

_____ 13. Each of the students found their room without any difficulty.

_____

_____ 14. If a person, who isn't used to exercise, runs five miles, he may be in trouble.

_____

_____ 15. When they had enlisted in the army, many new regulations to follow.

_____

_____ 16. That you are angry with your new boss doesn't surprise me.

_____

_____ 17. They say that ivory soap floats because it is so pure.

_____

_____ 18. To go into the forest so soon after all that rain, would have meant getting wet.

_____

_____ 19. Surprisingly, neither the president nor the vice-president of our school chorus sing very well.

_____

_____ 20. The new cars are supposed to pollute less than previous cars, they have special emission-control systems.

_____

_____ 21. Elaine bursted into the room to show her mother the picture she had drawn at school that day.

_____

_____ 22. The dorm was noisy, the food was terrible, and the classes were uninstructive.

_____

_____ 23. The agency found children for potential parents who were up for adoption.

_____

_____ 24. My canary sings pretty whenever I walk into the room.

_____

_____ 25. The men in the office where I work every day gives me trouble.

_____

_____ 26. He is not a banker who I would trust with my money.

_____

B. One-Paragraph Essay Write a tightly organized paragraph on one of the subjects below. Circle the number of the subject you choose.

1. The men and women I know have very different ideas about sex.
2. If there is another draft, women will be called to serve their country right along with the men.
3. The welfare system keeps people poor.
4. The U.S. will have to come to terms with Third-World interests soon.

5. Supposedly, a college is an intellectual community.
6. The current energy crisis should engage the attention of all Americans.
7. The U.S. cannot compete on a serious basis in Olympic sports.
8. One of my friends has influenced me greatly.
9. Most men I know are male chauvinists, but they won't admit it.
10. Most women I know are female chauvinists, but they won't admit it.

_____

_____

_____

_____

_____

_____

_____

_____

_____

_____

_____

_____

Test: Section I. Basic Parts and Basic Problems

1. The Simple Subject

A. In the list below, circle each word or phrase that *can* be the subject of a sentence.

1. porcupines	11. Boy Scouts of America
2. Colonel Sanders	12. coolness
3. from	13. superior
4. serviceable	14. alarms
5. imagination	15. my Uncle Toby
6. deliver	16. jam
7. *Guinness Book of World Records*	17. pitted against Stalin
8. although	18. read a book
9. indirect	19. surprised by fear
10. silly	20. finally

B. In the spaces below, supply a list of words that can be subjects of sentences.

1. _____   6. _____

2. _____   7. _____

3. _____   8. _____

4. _____   9. _____

5. _____   10. _____

2. The Subject with Adjective Modifiers

A. Words that describe a simple subject help complete the meaning of the subject. The list below consists of simple subjects with adjective modifiers that describe the subject. Put a circle around the words that are *not* the simple subject. Your circles will contain adjective modifiers that describe the simple subject.

1. one unpleasant memory
2. my very best friend
3. someone's oldest shoe
4. Milwaukee's high scorer
5. starting again
6. Little Rita from Ontario
7. the next class
8. simple arithmetic
9. the song we heard
10. an active person

11. mean people indeed
12. sweet Elaine from next door
13. my humble beginnings
14. more than my earnings
15. his determination
16. Jasper's desire to vote
17. being absent from home
18. your final decision
19. a two-week vacation in Maine
20. love, like an old song,

B. Supply reasonable adjective modifiers for the subjects below. Add adjective modifiers before and after the subject.

1. _____ intelligence _____

2. _____ activities _____

3. _____ Juarez _____

4. _____ Luther Hamilton _____

5. _____ Standard Oil Company _____

6. _____ talent _____

7. _____ difficulty _____

8. _____ shame _____

9. _____ screens _____

10. _____ calls _____

3. The Simple Predicate

A. The simple predicate is a verb whose action is complete. Put a circle around the words in the list below that, by themselves, can be verbs in a sentence.

1. decide	11. Jerry
2. intended	12. style
3. place	13. dripping
4. alarming	14. sleep
5. will stand	15. did not lie
6. having put	16. was trying
7. would have said	17. would be sick
8. might	18. will have been named
9. having begun	19. shove
10. grasp	20. seashore

B. Underline the predicate verbs in the following sentences. If a verb is incomplete or is incorrect in any way, write the corrected form of the verb in the space provided to the left of the sentence.

_____   1. By the end of the tour he will have sung "America" many times.

_____   2. The children in the park swinging too high for their own safety.

_____   3. The bus driver swerve sharply to miss the deep pothole in the road.

_____ 4. The girl in the flowered dress and the wide-brimmed hat sank gracefully down into the deep, soft seat.

_____ 5. Emily has ate more doughnuts than anyone else at the dance.

_____ 6. In the bottom drawer of the third desk to the left sits a pile of important letters.

_____ 7. All of the customers in the supermarket were complaining about the poor quality of the food.

_____ 8. The nine o'clock train had stop to pick up several more passengers than usual that day.

_____ 9. The dog might have been protecting its owner at the time of the disaster.

_____ 10. Those students in the cafeteria be waiting a long time for their meal.

C. Write ten words below that can be verbs in a sentence. Use a variety of verb tenses: present, past, future, and any other you choose. Do not use any verbs from the list above.

1. _____   6. _____

2. _____   7. _____

3. _____   8. _____

4. _____   9. _____

5. _____   10. _____

4. The Predicate with Adverb Modifiers

A. In the sentences below, circle the words that are adverb modifiers. Do not circle the verb or helper verb (such as "was" or "have").

1. He finally knew the truth about that awful incident in the past.

2. Magicians with any concern for their reputation will never tell the secrets of their trade.

3. Ted Williams hit the ball harder than most other baseball players of his time.

4. My mother told me the story of Little Red Riding Hood long ago.

5. Immediately, the two men began to dig out the debris from around the cave-in at the mine.

6. The newly married young man went next door to his neighbor's house to borrow a cup of sugar.

7. Joe closed the door of his new car fast.

8. In the face of so many questions and complaints, Betsy wondered briefly about the value of her decision.

9. The fifteenth annual Memorial Day parade in Center City slowly continued to move.

10. Never again will Jim Wells drive sixty miles to get a loaf of bread.

B. In the spaces below write sentences that contain a good predicate verb with adverb modifiers. You may put the modifier before, after, or between the parts of the verb.

1. _____

2. _____

3. _____

4. _____

5. _____

6. _____

7. _____

8. _____

9. _____

10. _____

5. The Predicate with Objects and Complements

A. Most of the sentences below contain an object or a complement after the predicate. For each sentence, underline the predicate verb. Circle the object or complement, if there is one, and identify it in the space provided: O for object, NC for noun complement, and AC for adjective complement.

_____ 1. His many supporters in the district encouraged him to run for

City Council.

_____ 2. My friend John has been rummaging around in his desk for an

hour in search of a pencil.

_____ 3. In my opinion, Kate's boyfriend, Pete, was attractive in an

offbeat sort of way.

_____ 4. Out of all the runners in the city-wide contest, he was fastest.

_____ 5. At this rate he will have eaten twenty hot dogs by five o'clock

this afternoon.

_____ 6. Suad won't sit under the apple tree with anyone else but me

or her sister.

_____ 7. Phil was the leader of the band until recently.

_____ 8. Under the circumstances they would never have given him a

fair trial in that city.

_____ 9. Some teachers assign too many papers to be handed in over a

short period of time.

_____ 10. The President of the Student Council should have been the

defender of students' rights on that occasion.

Name _____ Date _____

6 and 7. Independent Clauses and Sentence Fragments

Some of the examples below are independent clauses, and some are sentence fragments. In the space at the left of each example write IC for independent clause and F for fragment as appropriate.

_____ 1. The many examples of outright slander printed in that awful newspaper daily.

_____ 2. Faith moves mountains.

_____ 3. The last moon probe was successful for many reasons.

_____ 4. Because my friend Sam had too many questions that couldn't be answered easily.

_____ 5. When the rain started to come down in sheets, Joe standing on the corner getting soaked.

_____ 6. Over against the tree that is third on the left after you pass Mrs. Flack's house.

_____ 7. All the physicians in the world can't cure a heartache.

_____ 8. If you don't see me at the game, it is because I had to stay home.

_____ 9. The baboons at the zoo very clever.

_____ 10. After all is said and done, women in America been voting indirectly for a long time.

8. The Run-On Sentence

Some of the sentences below are run-on sentences; some are not. If the sentence is correct, place a C in the space provided to the left. If it is a run-on, write the word that comes before the punctuation mark needed to punctuate the sentence, the punctuation mark itself, and the word that follows. The first example is filled in to show you how it is done.

_____drought; he_____ 1. The farmer left after the first drought he couldn't stand another crop failure.

_____ 2. In front of the burning apartment building stood a crowd of onlookers.

_____ 3. The spring weather filled Jan with energy, she even took up jogging again.

_____ 4. Fred's piano instructor, who worked with him for many years, has moved to Arizona.

_____ 5. Scott, who didn't like dancing, left the party, he went to a movie instead.

_____ 6. You can either eat your cake or you can have it, but you must make a choice, no one can do it for you.

_____ 7. If Ron does go to the game, which I rather doubt, he will have to bring his own chair.

_____ 8. At the end of a busy day Maida likes to sit down and rest.

_____ 9. The trees were ready to burst into bud
after the warm weather we had they put
forth leaves by the thousands.

_____ 10. If you are trying to get to Centerville, don't
go west, you should go south.

9. Subject and Predicate Agreement

In the following sentences, some of the verbs agree with their subject; some do not. In the space provided, place a C for correct subject-verb agreement or an I for incorrect agreement. If the agreement is incorrect, write the correct form of the verb.

_____ 1. Many people from our neighborhood in Brooklyn has gone wrong.

_____ 2. Discrimination against women is illegal.

_____ 3. The Vietnamese has endured hardships over the past several generations.

_____ 4. Each of the children are being asked to bring a friend along on the trip.

_____ 5. Across the street in the house with many windows live our teacher.

_____ 6. His collection of disco records sounds great.

_____ 7. Brian plays baseball, but the other boys play even better.

_____ 8. The crises has played an important part in the breakdown of communication.

_____ 9. The vendors in the old marketplace doesn't want to have to get a license.

_____ 10. Anybody who breaks these rules are asking for trouble.

10. Pronoun Agreement

In the sentences below, fill in the spaces with an appropriate pronoun. Underline the referent.

1. She is a woman_____I have admired for a long time.

2. Everyone should know_____own telephone number.

3. Sam told Elvira that she would have to bring_____own car to the affair.

4. Replace the book on the shelf_____is to the left of the library door.

5. All of the people in this room should have_____heads examined.

6. Jaime pointed out the salesperson_____had sold him the faulty merchandise.

7. The timing device for turning lights on automatically has _____ dial set for eight o'clock.

8. Each of the students in this class wanted_____own desk.

9. That wonderful movie,_____I had seen several times in the theatre, is finally coming to television.

10. If you had seen the clown_____I saw tap-dancing down the street, you would have laughed, too.

Test: Section II. Principles of Subordination

11. Subordinate Clauses: Time, Place, Action

A. Circle each subordinate clause in the list below.

1. My Uncle John

2. After the party at Ruth's house

3. Until you wept

4. When he spoke

5. Nobody had a dime

6. Expecting nothing more

7. Because of the rise in taxes

8. Designing houses

9. Every single nondetergent soap

10. Without a doubt

11. Until James said what he did

12. Tell us what happened

13. Larger than a Russian wolfhound

14. Even if Freddie told me himself

15. Unless the president says so

16. Willing to have me over

17. Since no one else could go

18. Precision help

19. While everybody slept

20. Near where we used to eat

B. Write your own subordinate clauses of time, place, and action below.

1. _____

2. _____

3. _____

4. _____

5. _____

6. _____

7. _____

8. _____

9. _____

10. _____

12. Subordinate Clauses: Nouns and Adjectives

Underline the clauses in the following sentences. Then, in the space to the left, tell whether the clause is a noun clause (NC) or an adjective clause (AC).

_____   1. Give the ice cream to the boy who is crying in the street.

_____   2. I will talk about whomever I please.

_____   3. That Val goes swimming every day after school is known to all.

_____   4. I don't know why you would want to involve yourself in his escapades.

_____   5. The book that May read yesterday was too adventurous for her taste.

_____   6. The winner will be the first one who runs around the track three times.

_____   7. Beauty is whatever each person considers it to be.

_____   8. My bicycle, which I chose for its color and speed, is falling apart.

_____ 9. His excuse for being late was that his alarm didn't go off.

_____ 10. He is not someone for whom I have much respect.

13. The Prepositional Phrase

A. The prepositional phrase consists of a preposition followed by the name of something. Any preposition, such as "to," "of," and "in," can begin a prepositional phrase. Identify the prepositional phrases below by circling them.

1. in my solitude

2. with my friend Jim

3. after you left

4. behind my barn

5. to heaven and back

6. disguising Jasper

7. from my buddy

8. to male chauvinism

9. up in Michigan

10. at my expense

11. for you alone

12. while I snored

13. when you called

14. why not write

15. see me later

16. do something

17. be patient today

18. within the time set aside

19. from hunger

20. for the birds

B. Write your own prepositional phrases in the spaces below.

1. _____

2. _____

3. _____

4. _____

5. _____

6. _____

7. _____

8. _____

9. _____

10. _____

14. The Participial Phrase

A. Identify the participial phrases below by circling them.

1. Trying again

2. Caught by Jasper

3. Relenting once more

4. Deciding against my will

5. Having enjoyed myself

6. Having been hit by Tammy

7. Before he was going away

8. Nearly signing the treaty

9. Singing the school song

10. Even after my speech

11. When he was buying a new toaster

12. Offended by what his brother had done

13. Ferdy was hurting himself

14. Brought down by hatred

15. Approved by the president himself

16. If he was asked by the press

17. Minding the store

18. Mistaken for another person

19. Not having a thing to do

20. Living near me

B. In the spaces below, write your own examples of sentences using participial phrases. Try to make them as varied as possible.

1. _____

2. _____

3. _____

4. _____

5. _____

6. _____

7. _____

8. _____

9. _____

10. _____

15. Infinitive Phrases

A. Some of the following sentences have infinitive phrases; some do not. Underline each infinitive phrase and tell how it is used (subject, adverb, and so on) in the space provided to the left.

_____ 1. I have promised to defend your right to attend the school of your choice.

_____ 2. To all of us here your attitude seems wrong.

_____ 3. His assignment was to pass out papers to each student.

_____ 4. Pat took a side street to avoid the confusion caused by the fire.

_____ 5. To be defined by my parents' attitudes makes me angry.

_____ 6. Sam tried to give a handout to the man walking hurriedly down the street.

_____ 7. To take my picture he was forced to step back several feet.

_____ 8. If you want to earn some money, go to the employment office in your neighborhood.

_____ 9. To the average person earning a living is important.

_____ 10. Norma went through many procedures to have her pass-

port verified.

B. Write your own sentences with infinitive phrases in the spaces below.

1. _____

2. _____

3. _____

4. _____

5. _____

6. _____

7. _____

8. _____

9. _____

10. _____

16. The Gerund Phrase

A. Some of the sentences below contain gerunds. Underline each gerund phrase and describe how it is used (subject, object, and so on) in the space provided to the left.

_____ 1. If you think hang gliding is easy, you should try it yourself.

_____ 2. Swimming rapidly away from the wreck, he tried to save himself from drowning.

_____ 3. The dress was made of alternating bands of blue and gold.

_____ 4. Being secretary of the Scribbler's Club involves long hours of work.

_____ 5. He was going to the ball game after he came home from school.

_____ 6. Mack doesn't like any sport except bowling.

_____ 7. Before repairing the radio, he was careful to protect himself by pulling out the plug.

_____ 8. Asking too many questions can sometimes get you into trouble.

_____ 9. Joyce thought that her favorite leisure time activity was probably reading the newspaper at the breakfast table.

_____ 10. Placing the stepladder next to the broken window, he climbed carefully.

B. Write your own sentences with gerund phrases in the spaces below.

1. _____

2. _____

3. _____

4. _____

5. _____

6. _____

7. _____

8. _____

9. _____

10. _____

21. Proofreading the Sentence

The following paragraph contains many errors. Proofread the paragraph, using the techniques discussed in Unit 21. Circle the part of the sentence that needs correcting, and then write your corrected version of the paragraph in the spaces provided below. For your convenience, the sentences are numbered. Use these numbers to identify the sentences in your rewritten paragraph. If there is no change, rewrite the sentence as it stands. The result should be a paragraph that has been carefully proofread and carefully rewritten.

(1) Most high school seniors, who have decided to go on to college, have many difficulties during the period between making this decision and actually being accepted by a school. (2) This is a time of great anxiety and tension. (3) The fact is that many schools require applicants to take the College Entrance Examination Boards. (4) Not only are the tests difficult the following wait for scores makes most students nervous. (5) If they score low, they may decide to take the tests over again, a painful decision. (6) The task of choosing the college to which to apply presents another problem. (7) Students are bombarded with brochures from all over the United States. (8) How is a student to know, which school is best for him? (9) Each student has to consider their areas of interest, he has to consider his parents' financial situation, and he has to consider his chances of being accepted, among other considerations. (10) Conferences with school counselors may be helpful, but ultimately the decision of where to apply is up to the student. (11) Of course, the worst anxiety of all comes after the applications are in, at this point,

there is nothing to do but to sit and wait. (12) The tension unbearable for some. (13) Those who receive their acceptances early are lucky; those who don't hear until the last minute, endure agonies of jealousy and despair. (14) Once applications have been answered, and the worst is passed. (15) Senior students can begin to deal with any disappointments they have experienced, and they can start making plans for the next fall. (16) But one thing is certain: anyone who says that the senior year in high school is a carefree time has never known a senior undergoing the trial of applying to college.

Name _____ Date _____

_____

_____

_____

_____

_____

_____

_____

_____

_____

_____

_____

_____

_____

_____

_____

Index

A 9
B 0
C 1
D 2
E 3
F 4
G 5
H 6
I 7
J 8